Mother Tongue

Mother Tongue

Demetria Martínez

ONE WORLD

BALLANTINE BOOKS • NEW YORK

Library of Congress Catalog Number: 96-96808

ISBN: 345-40602-8

Text design by Holly Johnson
Manufactured in the United States of America
First Ballantine Books Edition: September 1996
10 9 8 7 6 5 4 3 2

To the memory of the disappeared

I am indebted to iconographer Robert Lentz for his images of Archbishop Oscar Romero and the Mother of the Disappeared. Numerous Chicano and feminist scholars, including David Carrasco and Deena Metzger, have shed new light on the history of spirituality. I am grateful for their work. Finally, I want to thank my parents, Ted and Dolores Martínez, for their faith; and Mary J. Vineyard and Valentina Cruz Dixon, for knowing a story when they see one.

The characters in this novel are fictional but the context is not. More than 75,000 citizens of El Salvador died during a twelve-year civil war, which officially ended in 1991. Most died at the hands of their own government. The United States supported this effort with more than $6 billion in military aid. Declassified State Department documents indicate that officials at the highest levels of the U.S. government knew of El Salvador's policy of targeting civilians, including Archbishop Oscar Romero, who was assassinated in 1980. Those in power chose to look the other way.

Remember us after we are gone. Don't forget us.
Conjure up our faces and our words. Our
image will be as a tear in the hearts of those
who want to remember us.

—POPOL VUH, *MAYAN SCRIPTURES*

This is the story of how we begin to remember
This is the powerful pulsing of love in the
vein

—PAUL SIMON, "UNDER AFRICAN SKIES"

One

His nation chewed him up and spat him out like a piñon shell, and when he emerged from an airplane one late afternoon, I knew I would one day make love with him. He had arrived in Albuquerque to start life over, or at least sidestep death, on this husk of red earth, this Nuevo Mejico. His was a face I'd seen in a dream. A face with no borders: Tibetan eyelids, Spanish hazel irises, Mayan cheekbones dovetailing delicately as matchsticks. I don't know why I had expected Olmec: African features and a warrior's helmet as in those sculpted basalt heads, big as boulders, strewn on their cheeks in Mesoamerican jungles. No, he had no warrior's face. Because the war was still inside him. Time had not yet leached its poisons to his surfaces. And I was one of those women whose fate is to take a war out of a man, or at least imagine she is doing so, like prostitutes once upon a time who gave themselves in temples to returning soldiers. Before he appeared at the airport gate, I had no clue such a place existed inside of me. But then it opened up like an unexpected courtyard that teases dreamers with sunlight, bougainvillea, terra-cotta pots blooming marigolds.

It was Independence Day, 1982. Last off the plane, he wore jeans, shirt, and tie, the first of many disguises. The church people in Mexico must have told him to look for a woman with a bracelet made of turquoise stones because he walked toward me. And as we shook hands, I saw everything—all that was meant to be or never meant to be, but that I would make happen by taking reality in my hands and bending it like a willow branch. I saw myself whispering his false name by the flame of my Guadalupe candle, the two of us in a whorl of India bedspread, Salvation Army mattresses heaped on floorboards, adobe walls painted Juárez blue. Before his arrival the chaos of my life had no axis about which to spin. Now I had a center. A center so far away from God that I asked forgiveness in advance, remembering words I'd read somewhere, words from the mouth of Ishtar: *A prostitute compassionate am I.*

July 3, 1982

Dear Mary,

I've got a lot to pack, so I have to type quickly. My El Paso contact arranged for our guest to fly out on AmeriAir. He should be arriving around 4 p.m. tomorrow. As I told you last week, don't forget to take the Yale sweatshirt I gave you just in case his clothing is too suspicious looking. Send him to the nearest bathroom if this is the case. The Border Patrol looks for "un-American" clothing. I remember the time they even checked out a woman's blouse tag right there in the airport—"Hecho en El Salvador." It took us another year and the grace of God to get her back up after she was deported.

Anyhow, when he comes off the plane, speak to him in English. Tell him all about how "the relatives" are doing. When you're safely out of earshot of anyone remind him that if anyone asks, he should say he's from Juárez. If he should be deported, we want immigration to have no question he is from Mexico. It'll be easier to fetch him from there than from a Salvadoran graveyard. Later on it might be helpful to show him a map of Mexico. Make him memorize the capital and the names of states. And I have a tape of the national anthem. These are the kinds of crazy things la migra asks about when they think they have a Central American. (Oh yes, and if his hair is too long, get him to Sandoval's on Second Street. The barber won't charge or ask questions.) El Paso called last night and said he should change his first name again, something different from what's on the plane ticket. Tend to this when you get home.

I've left the keys between the bottom pods of the red chile ristra near my side door. Make yourselves at home (and water my plants, please). I've lined up volunteers to get our guest to a doctor, lawyers, and so forth for as long as I'm here in Arizona. God willing, the affidavit from the San Salvador archdiocese doctor will be dropped off at the house by a member of the Guadalupe parish delegation that was just there. That is, assuming the doctor is not among those mowed down last week in La Cruz.

As I told you earlier, our guest is a classic political asylum case, assuming he decides to apply. Complete with proof of torture. Although even then he has only a two percent chance of being accepted by the United States.

7

El Salvador's leaders may be butchers, but they're butchering on behalf of democracy so our government refuses to admit anything might be wrong. Now I know St. Paul says we're supposed to pray for our leaders and I do, but not without first fantasizing about lining them up and shooting them.

Now see, you got me going again. Anyway, we used to marry off the worst cases, for the piece of paper, so they could apply for residency and a work permit. But nowadays, you can't apply for anything unless you've been married for several years and immigration is satisfied that the marriage is for real. Years ago, when Carlos applied, immigration interrogated us in separate rooms about the color of our bathroom tile, the dog food brand we bought, when we last did you-know-what. To see if our answers matched. Those years I was "married" I even managed to fool you. That is, until we got the divorce, the day after he got his citizenship papers. But you were too young for me to teach you about life

8

outside the law. Which used to be so simple in the old days.

Failing everything, we'll get the underground railroad in place. Canada.

Thanks, mijita, for agreeing to do this. The volunteers will take care of everything (they know where the key is hidden), so just make our guest feel at home. Maybe take him to Old Town. After all, it's not everyone who lives on a plaza their great-great-etcetera-grandparents helped build. I'm glad you have some time, that you're between jobs. With your little inheritance, you can afford to take a few months off and figure out what to do with your life. But don't get yourself sick over it. I'm fifty and I still haven't figured it out for myself. Just trust the Lord, who works in mysterious ways.

I don't know how long I'll be in Phoenix. My mother's last fall was a pretty hard one, and if she needs surgery, I could end up here for the summer. Don't forget to feed the cats and take out the garbage. I'm slipping

this under your door so that if they ever catch
me, I won't have conspiratorial use of the
mails added to all the other charges I've
chalked up. Rip this up! Be careful.

Love & Prayers,
Soledad

P.S.: Take it from one who survived the
'60s. Assume the phone is tapped until
proved otherwise.
P.S. #2: And don't go falling in love.

A clairvoyant moment doesn't make moving into the future any easier. If anything, it is a burden because one must forget what one has seen and move on, vulnerable as anyone. As we drove away from the airport in my blue pickup truck, shyness ground words to dust in my mouth. All that kept me from choking on silence was a sweet downpour of notes from a wood flute, a Cambodian wedding song on the university radio station. He was not a North American— nothing in his manner indicated awkwardness about silence. As I recall, he looked straight ahead, watched the city break in two as we cut through it, driving very fast on the freeway. My Spanish was like an old car, parts missing or held together with clothes hanger wire, but it got me where I wanted to go. Scraping together some words at last, I asked this man who had fled his country, did the airline serve you peanuts or a meal? He said, both, but I couldn't eat. He said, the movement of the plane made me nauseated, almost as sick to my stomach as the time I breathed tear gas at the funeral of a priest that death squads shot and killed as he lifted the communion host.

I'm not sure, twenty years later, that he used the words tear gas. I didn't then know its Spanish translation and I don't know it now. But for the sake of the story, tear gas will have to do. You see, I am good at filling in blanks, at seeing meaning where there may have been none at all. In this way I get very close to the truth. Or closer still to illusion.

Soledad died many years ago, but I have her letters. He, too, is dead, but I have a tape recording of a speech he gave, the newspaper accounts of it, some love poems. El Salvador is rising from the dead, but my folder of newspaper clippings tells the story of the years when union members disappeared and nuns were ordered off buses at gunpoint, a country with its hands tied behind its back, crying, *stop, stop.* These and a few journal entries are all I have left to fasten my story to reality. Everything else is remembering. Or dismembering. Either way, I am ready to go back. To create a man out of blanks that can never wound me.

I said, we have to pick a name for you, one that you would answer to in your sleep. On the plane ticket you're identified simply as A. Romero. I said that, or something like it, in Soledad's kitchen where Zapata, Cuba, and Nicaragua libre posters stuck to her cabinets, postage stamps mailing her house through the twentieth century. The kitchen always smelled of Guatemalan coffee beans ground with almonds. Or sometimes the air was spiked with lime, tomatillo, and cilantro that women mashed in a molcajete made of porous volcanic rock. Nameless women who appeared at night and rose with the heaving of garbage trucks to cook, to make themselves strong before North Americans bundled them off to other houses, further north. A. Romero and I sat at an oval oak table where newspaper articles that Soledad had clipped leaked out of manila folders. All the wars that passed through her house ended in a fragile cease-fire at this table, where plates of black beans and rice steamed as refugees rolled corn tortillas like cigarettes. This is where A. Romero and I lifted blue pottery mugs of hot coffee to our lips like communion chalices.

He said, Roberto, Juan, any name will do. I said, why not Neftalí, or Octavio? I wondered, why not pan for gold, for something weightier than the silt of ordinary names like Robert and John. He said, in my country names turn up on lists. Or in the mouths of army officers at U.S. embassy parties. A few drinks later, someone, somewhere disappears. Pick an ordinary name.

His eyes wandered away from me and into the living room on the other side of a white adobe arch encrusted with arabesque tiles. The house was a forest of flea market furniture that Soledad had coaxed to a sheen with strips of flannel nightgown. A tape player and cassettes of Gregorian chants were set on top of a black baby grand piano, its keys shining like the whites of eyes. A bay window of beveled glass framed the yard—elms, fresh stubble of Bermuda grass, roses flaring like skirts of flamenco dancers. Soledad lived in the Valley in a house made of terrones, blocks of earth cut a century before from the banks of the Rio Grande. Shadows of cotton-wood leaves twitched on an adobe wall that marked off her quarter acre. The house looked like it had been cut out and assembled from pic-tures in architecture books Soledad piled on her coffee table—Islamic, Pueblo revival, Territorial, things made to last, solidities refugees could only dream of.

He said, any name you pick will do. I said, it's not my place to decide. I believe I told him a story then, a story I'd heard on the university radio station on the way to the airport. A Spanish expedition comes upon some Mayan Indians. The Spaniards ask, what is this place called? The Maya answer, uic athan, we do not understand your words. The Spaniards believe they have been told the place is Yucatán so they impose that name on the place, inflict it. Like Adam, they think God has given them the right to name a world. And the world never recovers.

He smiled, crescent moon, then pressed his mug to his lips as if to mold them back into proper form. Maybe I'm imagining things, maybe more time passed before we smiled back and forth. But everything happened very quickly, this is the amazing thing. From day one I looked for ways to graft a piece of myself onto him, to become indispensable. My gestures were perfectly timed, touching his hand, twisting my hair, excusing myself to touch up my lipstick—ordinary actions that would reverse the tides of my life as in the theories of physicists who say the dance of a butterfly can cause volcanoes to erupt.

Love at first sight, this is how I explained the urgency that would later shed its skin and reveal pure desperation. Some women fall in love in advance of knowing a man because it is much easier to love a mystery. And I needed a mystery—someone outside of ordinary time who could rescue me from an ordinary life, from my name, Mary, a blessing name that had become my curse. At age nineteen, I was looking for a man to tear apart the dry rind of that name so I could see what fruit fermented inside.

This is what happened back then to women who didn't marry or have babies, who quit going to Mass. They begged to differ. They questioned their own names.

He picked the name José Luis.

Twenty years later, his name is a lens that allows me to see him as if for the first time. Five feet, five inches tall. Hair black as a pueblo pot. A scar above his right eyebrow, a seam sealing some old wound. His almond eyes were welcoming as windows open to spring, no screen, white curtain fluttering. But the rest of his face, with its hard jaw and serious mouth, was boarded up like a house whose owner knows what strangers can do when they get inside. Alert and polite, he always looked for ways to be of help. Before long he would be making coffee, taping grocery lists to the refrigerator, feeding the cats. But attention to detail was also a spiritual exercise to divert demons of exhaustion, I'm sure of this now. He had the hands of a man who had picked coffee or cut sugarcane for forty years. I'm not sure when he told me he was twenty-nine years old. By then it was too late. I had already counted the tree rings around his eyes and fallen in love with a much older man.

We must have gone down to Soledad's basement, must have heard steps creak as our soles adjusted the lower vertebrae of the house. But it is the smell I recall most clearly, the odor of damp earth, adobe walls maybe, or else just laundry swishing in the machine or hanging from a line that drooped above us like an eyelid. Red chile ristras hung from a rib cage of pipes over the door to José Luis's room. Dusty sunlight from an above-ground window touched down and lit up the objects in the room in a kind of still life: a bed with a blue Mexican blanket, chest of drawers, night table with lamp shade over a yolk of light, and a black pot blooming with dried chamisa.

He said, I don't need much space, all I have are poems and a Bible. He pulled these out of a shoulder bag, put them on the chest of drawers. His face suddenly grave, he surveyed the bed as if he feared someone might be hiding beneath it. Soledad had left running pants and a Harvard T-shirt on the pillow with a note, "For Our Guest." I translated it for him, only dimly sensing the depths of the conspiracy I was entering into, a pact to make him into someone else entirely. We were to shield him from the authorities by way of a fiction, a story that would obscure the truth rather than clarify it. It's amazing, looking back, to think that a few miles away a law library had books that were filled with words like aiding, abetting, transporting. Surely I knew the dangers. Yet surely wrongdoing was at the root of the thrill for a Catholic girl who had indulged in sex for the first time the year before, who had learned that breaking the law is a pleasure more poignant than sex itself.

Yes, from the very beginning I wanted him. In that time of my life, men were mirrors that allowed me to see myself at different angles. Outside this function, they did not exist. It was a supreme selfishness, the kind that feeds on men's attentions, a void flourishing in a void. José Luis would have none of it. When desire flickered across my face, he extinguished it with talk about El Salvador, the civil war, death squads, landowners. His struggles were too large and unwieldy to be folded up and dropped into my palm like alms. In the end, I had no choice but to love him. Desire was not good enough. Love would ripen in the light of time we spent together, like an arranged marriage. Except that I was doing the arranging. And calling it fate.

Weeks or months after his arrival, he asked

me, do you want to know my real name? I said no. No. I feared the authorities. But even greater than fear was my need for him to remain a stranger, his made-up name dark glasses he must never take off. Because making love with a stranger is always good. Even if you've known that stranger for a very long time.

July, 1982

Let me be
the bridge,
those troubled
waters,
his eyes,
~~Let me be~~

He's the most wonderful man I've ever met (and gorgeous too), this José Luis Romero. I swear to God the moment I laid eyes on him I knew he was The One. And it can't be a coincidence—that he arrived on the scene just as I was asking the universe whether or not there was more to life than just holding down boring jobs. I'd been so depressed. Now everything has changed. Still, I know I should slow these feelings down. Or else I'll want to act on them—which always ruins everything. I've got to remember I can't "make" anything happen beyond doing the footwork for some greater purpose that may be trying to manifest here. Maybe I'm supposed to just be his friend. Anyway, I don't know anything about that awful war he fled. Maybe it's better. He needs a friend who can just make him forget.

As for me, since he got here last week I have gotten up every morning feeling overjoyed. The usual guilt that bombards me whenever I wake up and try and enjoy my coffee while reading the classified ads has disappeared. I don't care anymore—not about getting a job or setting a schedule. In the mornings I actually enjoy choosing my clothes and putting on my makeup before driving to Soledad's. This morning a volunteer has taken him to meet with a lawyer and so I'm just sitting here listening to Gregorian chants and writing in this blank book I bought yesterday. It's like I'm going for longer and longer periods of time forgetting I'm depressed. Which maybe is a definition of happiness.

Unexpected things are happening to me. Like yesterday—I loaded up my truck with cans and wine and beer bottles, then went looking for the recycler's on North Edith. I stopped to get gas. And for some reason the smell of gasoline brought back memories of springs past. On KALB they were playing every bad but beautiful '70s love song you could imagine. Before I knew what was happening I got back in the truck and drove to Kmart on Candelaria. I had maybe five dollars in my jeans

pocket, but I couldn't stop myself—I
bought a black bra. The man hasn't even
kissed me yet. It was on sale. The blue
light special. The store siren went off and
I and all the other nuts pushing shopping
carts attacked boxes full of bras that
flapped around like crows as we grabbed
them and held them up for size. I even
bought nail polish (Aztec Red, 69
cents)—and this notebook.

Peace. Joy. Openness to the
future. How else can I describe what I'm
feeling except for the big "L" word,
which I don't dare say out loud. Because
it's like yelling fire in a theater. Men flee
and my girlfriends say to me, you fool.

Postcard of Old Town, Albuquerque: eigh-
teenth-century adobe plaza, shops with red chile
ristras on doorposts like Passover blood, Native
Americans selling jewelry under the portal in
front of the cantina. The picture must have been
taken after rain. The stucco surfaces of San

Rafael Catholic Church are the color of a bruised peach. The church is formidable, a battleship of adobe buttresses, dense walls and beams jutting around the top like cannons. A century ago an ancestor, Bernadina de Salas y Trujillo, helped make a soup of straw and mud to coat the church's outer walls. This fact seemed important to remember whenever I began to fall in love. When the spinning began and desperation set in, I reminded myself I am the descendant of women who did something useful with their hands, who knew what really mattered was to help shape something that would outlast their lives and their loves.

I rented a 100-year-old house with mud walls dark as a wasp's nest. It was across from the church, a few doors down from the cantina. Its walls were thick; I could sit in the low window frames of the living room or bedroom and watch the throngs of tourists. They were always taking pictures, an activity that reminded me of people who steal rocks from Indian ruins. I wondered if I would wake up one day and discover that Old

Town had disappeared. Before José Luis arrived, I often spent afternoons reading the Upanishads or the Tao Te Ching at the cantina, where a friendly bartender added wine to my orange juice at no extra cost. Like a homeopathic remedy, the dose acted on me in a way that was all out of proportion to its size. In a gesture of rebellion I mistook for dissent, I declared to myself that God could be found not just in a church but in a bar. I was nineteen, young enough to believe I had outgrown the walls of San Rafael Church. North American to the core, a consumer, I saw religion as a bazaar from which I could pick and choose. At the same time, I envied the women I watched leave morning and evening Mass, their faces wrinkled as ancient decrees. I wanted their faith, a massive doorway to stand under during life's earthquakes.

San Rafael's bells pecking away the shell of night. Tourists wielding cameras, machetes to tame their new wilderness. Shopkeepers hanging signs and drinking coffee in doorways from paper cups. Very often, when I try to remember those days, everything comes to mind except for memories of myself: what I looked like or said or felt. This is where it gets painful. You see, memory does not always serve me. It seeks images and feelings to hook on to, but at times encounters only voids. The facts are easy enough to recite. I quit college in southern New Mexico during my freshman year when my mother died. I returned to Albuquerque, held down a job at an escrow agency, then quit. During the years of my mother's illness, or maybe years before, I fled the world, went inside, ceased to feel. You could say I fell asleep. There was no mystery to it. Quite simply, it was easier to sleep and pretend to be awake than to stay awake and pretend to be strong. Twenty years later I can say this without shame. They had words for women like me. Insane fell out of favor as did nervous breakdown. Clinically depressed was, I believe, in vogue. But ask any woman who has had times in her life when she was not all there. She will say she was asleep.

And women who fall asleep and don't know why lack a plot line; this is the secret source of their shame. So I concocted a plot of my own, orchestrating what I could until characters began to say and do things I had never imagined, me included. To prove the gods at least were interested in me, I courted disaster, set out to love a man I knew full well would go away. Falling in love was a way of pinching myself. It proved I was alive if only on that thin line between drama and trauma. I handed my body over to José Luis like a torch to help him out of his dark places. I felt no shame. I was utterly unoriginal. To love a man more than one's self was a socially acceptable way for a woman to be insane.

Photograph of the Quaker Meeting House: A one-room school house in front of a barn, white with black trim, dice tossed in the middle of an alfalfa field. On the horizon, black clouds bloated with rain brush against the west mesa. I often visited the meeting house after José Luis went away and I ran out of ways to grieve. It was safe there, without hard edges, no altars or crosses or creeds, just respect for spaces as well as solids and a silence big enough for God. But on the night I am remembering now, pews creaked like an orchestra warming up as people greeted one another and sat down, talking excitedly. I was in the basement with José Luis. There were cots everywhere, and a sweet smell of almost-burned rice. A Guatemalan woman took a bandanna from her apron pocket and tied it around José Luis's mouth and nose. His eyes rose like little suns above the blue cloth. He adjusted it, then looked at her as if for assurance that he blended in—a refugee now, not a man.

It is that face, bizarre as an image in a tarot deck, that would appear in many newspaper photographs and evening newscasts. By the time he left Albuquerque, José Luis had told his story to a number of church groups. I was always there to tie the bandanna and eventually, I forgot why we were doing it and I ceased to be appalled. It all became normal. The half-moon of a face, camera lights brighter than the sun, his welcome "in the name of the Lord" to any immigration agent who might be in the audience. I always sat in the back of the room. After hearing his story once or twice, I stopped listening and tuned my thoughts to other, less painful frequencies. Someone was always available to translate for him, to catch his words in nets then let them out again.

"My name is José Luis Romero. I was born in Cuametl, department of San Juan in El Salvador. My father died when I was two years old. My mother washed clothes for the rich family—the village landowners—to support us. . . . In our colonia, among other problems, we lacked access to water other than the river. This situation came up in discussions at our Wednesday night Bible study group at the church. Father Gustavo had us reading and reflecting on the Beatitudes. Blessed the hungry, blessed the poor. Father Gustavo helped us to see that it was not God's will that we cross ourselves with holy water and die of thirst. Or take communion and starve. We decided that as a church project we would put in a communal well. There was even talk of starting a medical clinic with help from some Maryknoll nuns who were nurses. . . . The next Sunday we held Mass as usual. A friend of mine brought pupusas, which Father Gustavo used for communion because he said it reflected the people's culture. I tell you this because the Mass was the center of our village life. It was also where our village life, as we had known it, ended. I was standing in the back of the church when it happened. Father Gustavo lifted the sacred bread during the consecration and several shots rang out. Our beloved pastor died instantly, a merciful death. Two days later we found his sister, who was pregnant, cut up in pieces behind the church. I could tell you dozens of stories like that. . . . Before he was killed, Father Gustavo had helped me apply to the seminary in San Salvador. I wanted to pursue theological studies, perhaps become a deacon and serve in the provinces that have no priests. Father Gustavo even raised money for my tuition, appealing to some Jesuit friends in North America. I was there not even a full semester when I learned that some uniformed men had asked the dean where I could be found. He refused to say, and so the men went to my house in Cuametl and questioned my mother and grandmother. When I went there that weekend, my mother told me to get out of the country and not look back. . . ."

For twenty years I have stored the tape recording of his speech in a shoe box, his words ashes I couldn't bring myself to scatter. But last night he came to me in a dream, a blue bandanna covering most of his face. He took my hand and said gently, let me go. Let me go. As I write this, I am remembering that for a moment in the dream his hazel eyes became my eyes, clove-colored, lids powdered with brown shadow. When I woke up

I took the tape recording down from the closet and listened to his voice, a river still muddied with pain, transparent with conviction. Then I transcribed the tape. Pressing play and pause and play again, I listened to the melody of his words and wrote out the score. Afterwards I erased the tape, let silence dislodge his every word. I played it back to make sure everything was gone. It was like taking one last look around a hospital room where someone I loved had died. And I cried, I couldn't stop, it was a surprise. I thought my arroyo of grief had long ago dried up, leaving only an imprint of the storm.

Twenty years ago, quietly as a cat, he came up behind me as I sat at Soledad's piano, listening to the recording of his speech. It was morning; I thought he was still asleep. He said nothing, just listened, as if he might learn something new about his life in the retelling. But in those days, when a refugee told his or her story, it was not psychoanalysis, it was testimonio, story as prophecy, facts assembled to change not the self but the times.

I poured fresh coffee into our cups then showed him the article on the front page of the *Albuquerque Herald*, the photograph of his half-disappeared face above a swath of heads. Before I translated it I told him, the only thing they'll get right is that El Salvador is the size of Massachu-setts. I said, because your skin is brown, what you say will be followed by words like Romero claimed. Whereas if you were white, it would read, Romero said. That is how they disappear people here. Reporters aim cameras at you like Uzis. They insert notebooks and microphones between themselves and your history.

> ALBUQUERQUE, N.M.—In a
> speech blasting U.S. military aid
> to El Salvador, José Luis Romero
> (not his real name) told more
> than 100 church activists that he
> fled the Central American
> country because of so-called
> death squads.

Romero, who spoke last night at the Valley Quaker Meeting House, claimed that several of his seminary classmates had been murdered in San Salvador by the paramilitary organizations. San Salvador is the capital of the nation, which is about the size of Massachusetts.

Romero alleged that government authorities targeted the students because of their participation in a sociology class project aimed at identifying ways in which "the social fabric is affected when a few families own most of the land." Anyone who is critical of the ruling elites is in danger, he told the group.

"One by one, grass roots leaders in the shantytowns around the capital are being disappeared or killed. People are hiding their

Bibles," Romero said. "If you are caught with one, the authorities assume not only that you are literate but that you might press for change. The government wants us to go back to the days when the Kingdom of God referred to heaven only and not to what is possible on earth."

The 29-year-old man's face was covered with a handkerchief. Church activists told reporters that refugees' identities must be concealed to prevent harm to their families in their home countries.

According to several sources, dozens of Salvadorans and Guatemalans have stayed at the Meeting House as part of an "underground railroad" that helps them get to Canada. Activists claim such refugees are rarely

granted political asylum in the
United States.

Immigration sector supervisor
Jack Houston condemned the
gathering.

In a telephone interview, he
said church people who harbor
refugees or "put refugees on
display" are "advocating open
violation of the law."

"Those people are a
sanctimonious band of
renegades," Houston said.

Did I really say all that, about reporters? Was I
not, in fact, the one who read only the horoscopes, who looked to the stars to tell me what
God could not? José Luis was Aquarius, I Cancer.
His life was destined to be a statement about
the times; I was to suffer the times in my body.
His fate was to be a refugee; mine was to love
one.

July 1982

It was really awful hearing José Luis last
night at the Quakers'. I know shit like
that happens in the world, but why good
people get the bulk of it is beyond me.
In these past two weeks of hanging out at
Soledad's or running errands, he hasn't
said a word to me about what happened
to him in El Salvador—even though he'll
talk in a general way about what's
happening to the country. He goes out
of his way to be cheerful and helpful
around the house—he even draws doves
on notes he leaves me, telling me he's
gone off with a volunteer to see a lawyer
or to meet other refugees or whatever.

But last week, when he was
talking with a volunteer paralegal about
the ins and outs of asylum applications, I
caught a word or two that I knew had to
do with his past. Cell. Water. Cry. The
words had a barbed wire feel to them. I

didn't dare climb the fence to find out what was on the other side.

We heard some sickening things last night—but in the paper they didn't say much about the worst part. I told him you can't trust the media. Even Soledad, who's seen it all, tears at her hair every time she reads an article about El Salvador. I could tell he was pissed when I read him the piece. He clenched his jaws the way men do, crushing and swallowing his thoughts before they could get out. It's a shame the papers delete so much stuff. People would care more if they knew the whole truth. Soledad is always carrying on about how we have to change "social structures" in order to change the world. But frankly, I think you have to break a few hearts first—make people look ugliness in the face.

I wanted so badly to hold him last night. I couldn't help it. When we got

back from the Quakers' I went inside
and turned on the TV to see if anything
came out on the news. He went outside
and sat on the old elm stump, lit up, and
blew smoke rings at the moon. He
inhaled and exhaled like someone
catching his breath after almost drowning
in the ocean. If it weren't for the need to
breathe, he'd have been crying.

Meanwhile, I'm starting to figure
out part of the puzzle of this man. José
Luis is an Aquarius. The man's larger
than life. Which, unfortunately, is the
impression I have of most men. But he's
actually done something with his life,
tried to become a "subject, not an object,
in history" as he said the other day,
explaining "liberation theology" to me.
When he explained his philosophy of
life, my heart melted. It's wonderful to
feel this way about someone. And maybe
I can learn something from him,
something about faith.

Today's horoscope:

AQUARIUS: Higher profits are indicated. Bring yourself up to date on all tax and insurance matters. Overseas investments look more promising. Useful information comes from someone who works behind the scenes.

CANCER: Catch up on routine tasks. A long-distance telephone call will save you time and money. Continue to lay the groundwork for important moves you want to make in the near future.

August 5, 1982

Dear Mary,

Mijita, if you must lose your head over that boy, at least apply yourself and use the experience to shore up your Spanish. How do you think I learned English? Remember that good-for-nothing first husband I once told you about? Well, we were young and in love and what he said when we were together needed no translation. Falling in love with a man who

*speaks another language, you develop a third
ear. First, you struggle to understand what he
says. Then you begin to hear what he means.
Then the relationship falls apart. But you're
the better for it.*

*Me, I learned English because I had to. It
was not fun (until I met the good-for-
nothing). When I came up from Mexico I
gathered words like dung to fertilize life in this
alien land. And over time I fell in love with
English. Men? They came and went. But
the language is mine forever and ever.
Remember that.*

*I write this by the bluish light of my
mother's TV screen. My favorite Spanish
preacher is on, beamed in from Nogales.
Outside, there's a wild storm and a bad
feeling is in the air. Tonight when I opened
my Bible, my eyes landed on the passage from
Daniel: "And they that lead the many to
justice shall be like the stars forever." I know I
shouldn't read the Bible like tea leaves but
stars forever sounded like death to me. Not*

five minutes later, I got a call from my contact in Nogales. He said, "Archbishop Grande needs new vestments."

To make a long story short, the sheriff, who owes me one, brought over a bulletproof vest (I think they're called flak jackets nowadays) and pleaded with me not to tell him what I was up to. I told him the Lord would bless him, if not in this life then in the next one. To make a long story shorter still, my Nogales contact will take the vest to the Archbishop when he goes to San Salvador with a delegation next week. They say there may have been a massacre at the village of El Cordero and that the Archbishop is trying to get an investigation going. Which means he's in deep *you-know-what.*

Well, all this is neither here nor there. I'm so happy you and José Luis are getting along. It's good that between the volunteers and household chores and your "hanging out" together, he is developing a routine. Structure does wonders for people. (Thank him for

taking over my vegetable garden.) All I ask is
that when he's not looking, sprinkle his shoes
with holy water. I've been worried ever since
you told me he told you his pair belonged to a
compañero the treasury police gunned down.
The water will bless the footsteps of the living
and *the dead. Write soon—in Spanish. If*
you don't know a word, make it up.

Love & Prayers,
Soledad

It wasn't long after we met that he began introducing me to his favorite poets, copying in his notebook passages that meant something to him by writers like Pablo Neruda and Roque Dalton. It became obvious to me that poetry was his life. In the throes of apparently meaningless suffering, he lit it and smoked it and passed the sacred pipe to his friends until a new vision came to them about their earthly mission. Of course, this is clearer to me in hindsight. Because whenever he let me see what he had copied down, all I could conclude was that his heart, in advance of his mind, was trying to make contact with me. Trying to say I love you through the subversive valentines of great poets. We taped his jottings on the refrigerator where Soledad posted recipes, to-do lists, and prayers. I would not understand the sentiments actually expressed in those words until much later when I understood love could not be divorced from history, that his war had to become my war.

"Honor of the revolutionary poet: to convince his or her generation of the necessity for being revolutionary here and now, in the difficult period, the only one that has the potential to be subject of an epic. . . . to be so when the condition of being revolutionary is usually rewarded with death, that is truly the dignity of poetry. The poet takes then the poetry of his or her generation and gives it over to history."

—ROQUE DALTON

MORTALLY WOUNDED

When I woke up
this morning
I knew you were
mortally wounded
that I was too
that our days were numbered
our nights
that someone had counted them
without letting us know
that more than ever
I had to love you
you had to love me.
I inhaled your fragrance
I watched you sleeping
I ran the tips of my fingers
over your skin
remembered the friends
whose quotas were filled
and are on the other side:
the one who died

a natural death
the one who fell in combat
the one they tortured
in jail
who kicked aside his death.
I brushed your warmth
with my lips:
mortally wounded
my love
perhaps tomorrow
and I loved you more than ever
and you loved me as well.

—CLARIBEL ALEGRÍA

I've saved these jottings in my shoe box; the lead pencil letters are dark and fresh as new stubble on the face of a lover. The word *mortally,* smaller than the others, appears to have been written in a hurry. José Luis always spoke slowly and deliberately but with the passion of a prisoner imparting final instructions before a mass escape. The words in my old notebook, by contrast, look like they were written in a giddy stupor, the letters lassos with which I struggled to rope in feelings that galloped off in no clear direction. While José Luis was copying the works of revolutionaries, I was poring over Eastern mystical texts, discovering the meaning of life, for the moment at least, in gods incarnated as elephants and monkeys and many-breasted goddesses.

Here's a page from my notebook. No doubt I believed at the time that one or the other passage contained the sum of human wisdom.

> The clouds give of their substance
> The earth receives and renews,
> Within the body of the earth
> new bodies take root.
> Love between a woman and man
> is of the same order.
> Indeed, one self-forgetting act
> of giving and receiving renews
> the gods' hopes for creation.
> Their weeping ceases and they

wonder why they ever spoke
of bringing the world to an end.

A Zen Tale

"Is there anything I can do to make
myself Enlightened?"

"As little as you can do to make the
sun rise in the morning."

"Then of what use are the spiritual
exercises you prescribe?"

"To make sure you are not asleep
when the sun begins to rise."

It is difficult to recall the day-to-day exchanges
that became bridges by which we transcended
borders of culture, language, and history. We
strolled back and forth into one another's worlds,
or at least the outskirts of those worlds, as casually
as if crossing from El Paso to Juárez to buy liquor
or pharmaceuticals. In exchange for my driving
him around, he offered to help me with my
Spanish. Almost every day we sat together at the

kitchen table where we conjugated Spanish verbs with an old grammar Soledad had brought with her from Mexico. I was young, future tense came naturally to me: Iré, irás. . . . I will go, you will go. I have always lacked talent for living in the here and now, and back then I was easily transported into luminous, unobtainable futures. There were days I dreamed I would not only marry José Luis, but that we would buy a little house in the Valley, live on black beans and tortillas, and aid la revolución with computer bulletins to Central America. Whenever I took off on the runway of daydreams, always about José Luis, he playfully tugged at my braids and said, "Mary. Mary, can you hear me?" I remember how this little custom became another "sign" I took to mean he was falling in love with me. Everywhere, signs cropped up. And I hoarded them, rose petals I stashed between the pages of my days.

Still another custom evolved that made me feel he was carrying me over the threshold to a life more

spacious than the one I inhabited: late evenings on the couch, swirling spoons of molasses in
black coffee, and talking about la revolución in
Nicaragua. Don't ask me what I said. I couldn't
have cared less about politics. I was of that generation that held to some vague theory about how
hearts must change first; we had the luxury of
being able to think that way, and maybe there's
some truth to it. José Luis must have found it
charming. Both of us were, after all, dreamers.
José Luis's great misfortune was that he and his
compañeros had tried to put flesh on their dreams,
make them breathe. They counted them as bless-
ings and paid with their lives.

Here are more items I saved in the shoe box:
    A prayer Soledad copied from Our Lady's
    Prayer Book and mailed to me with
    instructions to repeat it at least three times
    each day.

    *I am anxious, dear mother, to be gainfully
    employed in work that will relieve my temporal*

needs without in any way endangering the spiritual well-being of my soul.

And a grocery list—my handwriting:
>Salsa ingredients (tomatillos, onion, green chiles, serranos, cilantro)
>Pupusa ingredients (masa de maíz, 1 lb. black beans, 1 lb. mozzarella)
>French green clay masque
>*Albuquerque Herald*
>Cat food
>Garbage bags
>Condoms

Soledad had a saying: Reality is a lump of clay and prayer is the potter's wheel. I believed her, because by late July or early August, not long after she called to say she was praying for us, both José Luis and I found part-time work in Old Town. He washed dishes at the cantina where the owner had no qualms about hiring "illegals";

he paid less than minimum wage but always in cash and on time. I covered for the owner of a bead shop when she was on buying trips. I sat behind a glass counter that held miniature jade Buddhas and amethyst prayer beads from Tibet. I remember fixing my attention on these objects and inhaling to the count of two, holding my breath to the count of seven, then exhaling as I counted one, two, three. My chest rose, froze, and fell in a triangle of attention that I undoubtedly learned about in books on Eastern mysticism. But whatever in me that may have actually aspired to enlightenment, to being in the present, did not bear up for long. I began using the tantric technologies to outwit the heat rather than embrace it. And when that failed, I daydreamed about autumn. But the fantasy was impossible to sustain.

The summer of 1982 still sounds like ice crunching between teeth, still looks like church bulletins folded into fans. The sun was red as a black widow's hourglass, and Old Town floundered in webs of heat. Nights were hot as cast iron; it was hard to hear anything above the cicadas. Even in the early mornings, the sky sparkled in a way that was not natural, like a vacant lot glittering with broken glass. After my shifts at the bead shop I always walked over to the coolest spot by the plaza kiosk to wait for José Luis—a cement bench under the sycamores where I watched the rites of summer. Touching stucco walls, shopkeepers gauged the heat's advance as if feeling a child's forehead for fever. Old women left Mass and scanned the heavens for signs of rain, shielding their eyes from the sun in a limp salute.

As the twin steeples of San Rafael pierced the sky and more hot air leaked into the world, the old men of the area flocked to benches on the plaza, their canes feeling the turf in front of them like trunks of elephants. They wondered aloud, as they did every year, whether the heat was not a sign from God, a punishment for having sold so much land to the gringos from back East. Brilliantine heads nodded and shined. The men fanned themselves with wilted newspapers while above them the flags of Spain, Mexico, and the United States snapped in false breezes. The old families of the area had endured the heat as they had so many sovereignties; they changed what they could and waited out the rest, forging over iced tea a solidarity that outlasted kings and seasons.

After finishing his shift at the cantina, José Luis sometimes crouched under the portal to look at silver and turquoise laid out on blankets in long furrows. He used to linger at the rug of a Navajo woman who sat on a precarious throne of milk crates as she awaited the day's harvest of tourist dollars. Now and again, groups of tourists engulfed her, cutting off my view of José Luis. This used to unnerve me. The Border Patrol had recently opened an office, declaring Albuquerque a border town—a city like El Paso or Browns-ville, ordered to empty its pockets and produce its documents. I feared if I lost sight of José Luis, the Patrol might take him away in one of its avocado-colored vans. And they could have, easily; they were armed to the teeth. I believed that watching José Luis generated protective forces; I vaguely remember some Eastern texts I was reading about the power of mindful observation—ironic, given that sight was my least evolved sense. Where others saw indigo, I saw blue; where others saw teal, I saw green. It's the draining away of color that happens in a woman's life when she can't name her own reality. It is only now that I am able to go back and color in the pale places, creating a mural on the walls of the life I now inhabit.

To track José Luis, I developed a sixth sense. Scanning the sea of tourists, I managed to latch onto a white patch of fabric among earth-toned clothing the better-off tourists ordered that year from the Banana Republic catalogue. His swatch of T-shirt became a kind of hologram that revealed the whole of him to me in three dimensions. And I held to that vision until the tourists moved on, their purchases made, cameras banked with images of a "real" Indian. Looking back now, I wonder what troubled me more, the fear that the Border Patrol might see José Luis or that the tourists in his midst could not see him, at least not in three dimensions. No, he was very dark, a dishwasher, an illegal alien. Had he spoken English, it would not have mattered; he still would lack the credentials pinned on those with British or French accents. All over the city refugees were rendered invisible with each stroke of the sponge or rake they used to clean motel rooms and yards and porches. Unlike wealthy refugees who fled their pasts and bought homes in Santa Fe, people like José Luis lacked the money to reinvent themselves. So they became empty mirrors. A ghostly rustle of Spanish spoken in restaurants above the spit of grease on a grill.

I still have the ring, a simple silver band, that José Luis bought from the Navajo woman. He gave it to me, said it was just a small gift to thank me for being his friend. Years later, I gave it to a psychic who ran her fingers over it and said she saw a man with a scar on his forehead who was saying, I will return. Last night I took the ring from the shoe box and held it, my eyes closed, until I, too, saw José Luis: We were making love on a bed in a basement. I slipped the ring on, inhaled, and counted to seven. And I arrived at that stillness so absolute the chaotic fragments of one's life arrange themselves, if only for a moment, into a mandala of meaning. On the exhale I remembered that José Luis was the first man to touch me in a way that I could feel real pleasure, could feel my flesh yield up its own indivisible truth.

I was leaning against the white railing of the kiosk when José Luis came to me and said, this is for you. The ring fit only on my wedding finger; the fingers of my right hand have always been stronger and slightly larger around. I tried to say something, tried to crack the silence, but it was like taking aim at a piñata, blindfolded. I could not manage even a simple thank you. At last I said, We're married, no?, to la revolución. Yes, why not, he said as a smile swept across his face, dusting off the traces of fear that marked him. I knew at that moment that José Luis was seeing

and wanting all that would come between us.
I remember this now, as I stroke the ring,
remember how he opened the door.

The Sandia Mountains, true to their name,
ripened at daybreak, the color of watermelon.
Here is a postcard of the Sandias, this is how they
looked one early morning when José Luis and I
were loading up Soledad's brown station wagon.
Two friends of hers were borrowing it for a
fishing trip. Roped to the top of the car, a canoe
extended over the windshield like the beak of an
eagle. Fishing rods poked out of windows like
antennae. One of Soledad's friends—they did not
tell us their names—adhered a Reagan-Bush
sticker to the car's back bumper. In those days,
the Border Patrol did not stop cars with Reagan-
Bush or Right-to-Life stickers on them. Nor did
the Patrol stop and question white men. In my
memory, one of Soledad's friends that morning
had blond hair and wore horn-rimmed glasses.

Back then, when "fishing trip" meant transporting refugees north, a white man was an asset. Millions of years of genetic coding culminated in a kind of liturgy each time a Border Patrol agent waved him past the checkpoint outside El Paso.

I'm trying to remember how it is that, after Soledad's friends drove away, José Luis kissed me for the first time. It is like trying to take snapshots twenty years too late. At least I recall the smell— the sage we burned in a seashell for Soledad, who had called to say she had forgotten to bless the house before she left. If only I could follow the wisp of sage back in time to the moment. . . . The truth is, some of our tenderest moments are the ones I am least likely to remember. It has to do with what I said about sleep, how women like me sometimes flee, letting loving words or glances melt on the hot pavement of some nameless fear.

So forgive me if I embellish; even a conjured memory is better than no memory at all if you would dare to give your life what the world did not, a myth, a plot. Besides, I never intended to reconstruct him from memory, just from love, which may be the only way anyone can ever hope to get at the whole truth. So let me say what might-have-been and maybe the facts will break through.

We are sitting cross-legged on Soledad's paisley couch facing one another and drinking coffee out of the blue mugs. I see a man who is not the same one I met weeks earlier at the airport. He is talking about rumors he picked up from the other dishwashers, about how easy it is to cross into Canada and to ask for a lawyer, to apply for political asylum. He says several of his coworkers invited him to join their soccer team, the best in the city, made up of Guatemalans and Salvadorans. It was amazing to me, how José Luis had salvaged the makings of a life out of fate's refuge heap. Earning money, teaching me Spanish, helping Soledad's friends translate human rights alerts: His activities gave him the confidence of a man who pokes a bonfire with a stick, dignified by the skill of generating light and heat.

60

He asks, have you ever kissed a man whose name you did not know?

I say, I knew the name but not the man.

I am trying to escape into abstractions, to speak with an authority all out of proportion to what I am actually saying. To dazzle him so he won't hear my heart galloping. I am about to get what I want and a rope of panic is stretched out before me as I run toward desire. I'm all stutters and sweat and clashing colors: purple pants, a green Lady of Guadalupe T-shirt. I'm afraid, after sitting cross-legged for so long, that my big toe will curl up in a cramp, my body an unruly cowlick. Then, he thanks me, yes, this really happened. He thanked me for sharing my sleeping pills with him, for making up a social security number based on numerology. Acts of solidarity, he said, his hazel eyes smiling. He touched my arm and I laughed, sipped from the chalice of happiness the universe set suddenly before me. He said, I love it when you laugh. Yes, it was real laughter, the kind that makes fences inside you fall. And seeing his opportunity, he crossed yet another border. Sweet collision of lips and tongues. I tasted Kahlúa and chamomile and some other barely familiar herb, steeped and sipped in another lifetime.

Yes, I believe it happened that way; I feel joy *now* echoing in me, striking against the canyon walls of forgetting. Our faces floated above our bodies, helium balloons linked by static. Like a radio alarm clock, the cicadas started up. Time stopped. There began a never-ending August that, years later, I would remember every time I smelled the sea in a swamp cooler or tasted the sea in another man's mouth.

August 1982

He said he loves me. He said he *loves* me.
(I used to plead with my first boyfriend
to say it!) José Luis kissed me for the first
time, but what he said means even more.
It's happening just as I knew it was
meant to happen. Spanish lessons, a ring
that fits on my wedding finger, our
drives back and forth between Soledad's

and Old Town. But most important of all, the word love. Without it my feelings spill all over the place—and it's always me (and my friends) who have to mop up afterwards.

Now I have reason to improve my Spanish. I have a word and a way of life to conjugate: Quiero, quieres, quiere, queremos. . . . To want and to love, the same thing! God, make this thing last. Make it last. I sound crazed, I know, but with good reason. My period's due any moment, and I have found true love. The kind that pulls all of life in one direction. It's too much. Already, his presence in my life is helping me forget all the sadness (what was it about?) that pulled me down for so long before he came to Albuquerque. And with the power of love I'm going to help him forget, too. Help him to forget the war that he fled from, that he says he still dreams about.

This morning I woke up to the sound of San Rafael's bells, and I remembered yesterday. I felt a grin spread through my whole body, pure bliss. The thought of being with him forever is intoxicating. But I've got to be careful. I've got to stay in the present. The minute I get hung up on the idea of *forever,* on what will happen tomorrow, I ruin everything. For all I know, the universe could get scratched like a record groove. We might do nothing but repeat yesterday morning over and over—couch to coffee maker, coffee maker to couch. (Yet what a gift this would be!)

From the Tao Te Ching: Heaven is lasting and Earth enduring. The reason for this is that they do not live for themselves alone; therefore they live long.

We did not make love, that is to say have intercourse, for weeks. Something perversely Catholic kept our explorations above the waist, the old religion erotically charging the most humble expanses of skin. Inner elbow, collarbone, fingertips. We touched each other on Soledad's couch until 3 A.M. when the train's cry severed the night. It's late, we have to work tomorrow, he said. But I don't need sleep, I don't need food, just you, I answered. I unpeeled myself from him, removed myself like a bandage. The cruelty of limits stung: the need for sleep, food, a paycheck however small. If an hour were a house one could move into for good, I would have built a wall around the 2 o'clock hour, a brick wall arrayed against the disfiguring fury of the future. He playfully yanked at my hair and patted my cheeks as if plumping up a pillow. He said he worried I might fall asleep while driving to Old Town. I assured him I would not; after being with him I always tuned in to a rock station, volume full throttle. He took my hand and walked me through the portal where red chile ristras were suspended like tongues of fire. We opened a rotting wood gate that led to the front

yard. After I got into the pickup truck, he kissed me goodnight, lips and forehead, through the rolled-down window. If he asked me for a sleeping pill I gave him half of mine, snapping apart a chalky oval no bigger than an infant's thumbnail. I took a pill whenever emotions, good or bad, detonated, leaving a cloud of mental chatter I could not dissipate on my own. He said the pills helped him fall asleep after nightmares woke him up, causing his heart to race. It was as if our minds were satellite dishes, open to the murmurings of some dark universe. Signals bombarded us, signals we could not yet decode.

Then one day it happened, it happened. I love you, José Luis. Te quiero, María. We opened each other up like sacred books, Spanish on one side, English on the other, truths simultaneously translated. I remember the scent of our sweat, sweet as basil as we pressed against one another on the basement bed. Lindita, mamacita, negrita: love words, the kind that defy translation. With his hands he searched my depths. When he found what he was looking for I moaned, felt a chill and then warmth as the seasons moved through me. Minutes later he came inside me, stiffened, sighed. Afterwards, he lit his cigarette on the flame of the Sacred Heart candle on the night table. He rubbed my feet with almond oil, talked in the dark about developments in El Salvador. We had both dreamed the night before about his country. I said, José Luis, last night I dreamed I was there, I smelled bougainvillea. He said, I dreamed I was there too, mi amor, but it was something about white phosphorus, napalm.

He stayed awake, talked to me; I didn't feel the doubts women sometimes feel when men fall asleep after making love, doubts delicate yet dangerous as asbestos fibers. Sometimes we held one another and listened to the shortwave radio that we had brought down from its place on the kitchen window sill. I remember a BBC commentator saying something about South Africa, and how his descriptions shattered like crystal wine glasses at the sound of a woman crying out in grief. But the sounds diminished as our bed bobbed away on the tide of sleep. Holding on to José Luis, my head pinned to his chest, I held on to the night, refused to let it slip through my hands. There were times I felt sad after making love. Intercourse often disappointed me. It could feel like a linear fitting of parts, a far cry from the creative pleasures of foreplay when we painted on the caves of one another's flesh. Perhaps it would have been different had I wanted a baby. Maybe then the act, with its audacious committing of present to future, would have touched the flaming core of my being. But I'm deceiving myself again. Lying. For a long time after José Luis left me I continued to believe a man could touch my essence, make me whole. All that time I could have been writing, touching the fires of my being and returning to the world, purified and strong.

You see, I was one of those women who is at her best when she wants something very badly. The mating dance, the yearning and flirting, surrenders and manipulations—I was good at that, so good at the pursuit that when I actually got what I wanted, terror appeared. Terror that wore the silly mask of disappointment.

Here is a poem José Luis wrote, dated August 13, 1982. As part of a Spanish lesson, he had me translate it. We kept several dictionaries on the kitchen table. Dodging from word to word for hours at a sitting, we made our way across borders of language without passports or permits. I hid whatever poems he gave me in a sock drawer. The feelings his poetry engendered in me were like nothing I had experienced before. His words and those of the poets he admired made me want to sell my belongings, smuggle refugees across borders, protest government policies by chaining myself to the White House gate—romantic dreams, yes, but the kind that dwell side by side with resistance. The space we cleared on the kitchen table to do translations, near folders of clippings about El Salvador, was a magic circle. It was beyond law and order.

#1

night sheds her black silks
it is the first day of the world
love, lover
I uncurl your sleeping fist
your hands on my chest
yield up their aloes
scars recede
resplendent our flesh
no losers or winners
when wars end
just survivors
to lay hands
on one another
to begin again

—JL ROMERO

Around the time of José Luis's arrival, large numbers of U.S. citizens were beginning to make
trips to El Salvador in groups called delegations.
They met with sisters and priests, unionists, students, those who worked the land—anyone

whose life the government had deemed dispensable, that is to say poor people, most of El Salvador's population. And when delegations returned to the States, members spoke to anyone who would listen, in parish halls, homes, and on campuses. José Luis and I were among those who attended these presentations. I got good at whispered translations, rapid-fire summaries. Sometimes, exhausted, I reverted to Spanglish. I sprinkled Spanish words about just so, like dots in a connect-the-dot puzzle, and José Luis made the connections, discerning the full shape of the speaker's intent. What I did not need to translate, however, was the grief in the voice of a U.S. citizen who went to El Salvador to learn about la situación and who came away with a memory of evil. Innocence was lost time and again in this fashion, leaving a void that would be filled with either forgetting or anger, an anger embodied very often in commitment.

A priest who had traveled with an Albuquerque delegation came back with bullet casings imprinted with the name of a U.S. city—I can't

recall which one—where they had been manufactured. A month or so later the cleric gave
away his possessions and returned to El Salvador
for good, to work with the poor. These were not
isolated incidents but formed what became a
movement of sorts, of U.S. citizens taking an
"option for the poor," which liberation theolo-
gians said was God's way of acting in history.
These conversions could be traced to the stories
of Salvadorans, stories about torture, dismember-
ment, hunger, sickness. I heard those stories and
felt lucky. I had lost a mother to cancer and a
father to infidelity. My losses were natural. Or so
I thought then.

After a delegation member spoke one evening at San Rafael church, José Luis and I went
outside and, sitting on the steps of the kiosk,
watched fake gas lamps light up one by one. The
setting sun added a bronze lacquer to the adobe
walls of Old Town's shops. Folding their wool
blankets, Native Americans loaded up pickup
trucks with cartons of jewelry. José Luis took my
hand and pressed it to his lips. Then, he yawned

and stretched, reaching for the last rays of sun with forearms that had grown strong from washing dishes for endless afternoons. He took my hand again, traced the creases in my palm. For no reason I could discern, he looked at me and asked if he could call me María. I said of course, it's just Spanish for Mary. He said no, Mary is English for María.

The few friends I had during that spell of my life quit calling; the word must have gotten out that Mary was in love. They knew I wouldn't come out of the house, the house I drew with crayons, a house of primary colors I called love. The first time I fell in love, friends tried to tell me it was not real. To prove them wrong, I drew a keyhole on the front door and invited them to look through to the other side. See for yourselves, I said.

August 1982

I can't stop dreaming of marrying José Luis. It only makes sense. Marriage would be a way to kill two birds with one stone; I could save him from being deported *and* help him begin, at last, a new life. I could make something useful out of my life—and give myself some structure and direction while I'm at it. Besides, I practically live with him as it is. We're either hanging out at Soledad's or going back and forth to Old Town. He's getting pretty regular work now at the cantina. (He met some other refugees there, including a guy from his own village.) The plaza's like a third home to him, after Soledad's and after Salvador.

Heck, maybe we should just move in together. It would make things a lot easier. We wouldn't have to spend half our lives in the truck. We could spend more time doing poetry translations, which is when he seems happiest. The problem is I don't know if I could really bring myself to believe in living together. Because I still believe in marriage—no matter how many tries it takes to get it right. Though most people my age, last I heard, tossed marriage out along with the flat-earth theory. It's embarrassing. Once a Catholic always a Catholic. You rebel and rebel against the Church's stupid rules, but the fact is, you wouldn't bother to rebel if you didn't believe in your heart of hearts that there was something worth rebelling against.

Even Soledad says if she ever gets married a fourth time, she'll get one of her radical Jesuit priest friends to do the wedding. Besides, living together seems so ordinary nowadays. (And my life has already been too ordinary!) And Old Town is still an old-fashioned little village. If word got back to old Mr. Baca that the girl he was renting to was living in sin (across from the church at that), who knows what might happen? I still worry about what people think—as if they didn't have their own secret sins. It's ridiculous.

(But if by some miracle José Luis and I do get married, I want to write my own vows. It's dangerous for a couple to promise to stay married until they die. It's better to vow to stay together until the marriage dies—and to do everything in their power to keep it alive. If you don't think of marriage as a plant, fragile and in need of attention, then you're asking for major trouble.)

I'd better get over to the cantina. José Luis will be off his shift, and we can get beers at this time for half price. We've gotten in the habit of going there in the afternoons. It's really beautiful. Ancient wooden saints stand in niches in the adobe walls. Candles burn every-where. We feel safe there. He told me that in the darkness, with the santos, no one can tell he's an illegal. I told him no human being on earth is illegal. He accused me of being romantic again and said, go tell that to the authorities.

One thing that worries me is he's been drinking a lot lately.

Every afternoon last week he finished off something like five beers in a sitting. I told him it's not good to drink that much, and he cut back to two beers or so when we went back the next day. I think he did it not because it's good for him but to please me. I don't like that. It's all to the same end, but I don't like the means. When I'm most centered I want him to put his needs above mine. That's what I hate about love. Bit by bit you start to give things up. You become like a good parent. But I love him so it's all worth it. I've never felt this way about anyone.

Two

August 5

I wish there were a way I could tell her. Say to María, you're inventing José Luis. And your invention may be very different from who I really am. She sees my scars and thinks I was brave for having survived. She doesn't understand that you don't always need to be brave to survive the most brutal injuries. Unfortunately (or fortunately?), wounds

will often start healing even if you don't
want them to, even if you would rather
die quietly in the corner of a cell. The
body's will to live sometimes is greater
than that of mind or spirit.

I wish I could say to her, nothing
I have done has required courage. When
you're being shot at, it doesn't take
courage to duck. Animals do as much.
Me and my compañeros were being shot
at so we dived for cover. And when we
were not dodging bullets, we were
asking questions about who made and
sold the bullets, who bought them, and
why they always end up in the hearts of
poor people. We tried to figure these
things out, to use our minds, our reason.
Me and my seminary classmates are
people of the book. Bible readers. Our
cry has been, not by the gun but by the
Word made flesh in action. How naive it
sounds now. Like a dream of poets and

would-be mystics writing in blank
notebooks in far away North America.

If there is courage to be found,
maybe it is in the hearts of those who
have headed for the mountains with guns
of their own. The rebels feed the people,
teach them to read and write. But they
also teach them to defend what they
have gained. That is the courage of
choosing not to be a martyr. I thought I
had made that choice, too, by coming
here. And by day, when I am speaking to
the other dishwashers about their
situation, or helping volunteers translate
human rights alerts, I know I am doing
the right thing. Using words to educate
people who have the power to influence
the U.S. government. But at night, when
I can't sleep, the torture starts up. I think
of friends sleeping under ceiba trees or
on dirt floors in cement block cells. I am
tormented, wondering if I did the right

thing. Or if I should be in my country, fighting. With words. Or with guns.

Sometimes the torment is so great that I turn to María for sleeping pills or sex or both. Sex to escape or at least to get me breathing again, to stop the cold shaking inside. And the next morning I have to live with my guilt at having used her. It wouldn't be bad if she just loved sex. But she loves me.

Or perhaps what she really loves is the idea of me. A refugee, a dissident, spokesman for a cause she knows little about, ignorance she seems to have made her peace with. She is trying to separate me in her own mind from my history. She thinks by loving the "real" me, the me before the war, she can make my memories of the war end. It is so American. The belief that people can be remade from scratch in the promised land, leaving the old self behind. I really think she believes if she loves me enough the scars inside me will disappear.

And in my own imperfect way, I love her too. I love her for believing that I can be whole, for loving me even if I exist largely as a figment of her imagination. My María with a heart as big as this house.

She makes a big deal out of the fact that I read the Bible. She says she has "fallen away" from the spiritual life. I hate it when she talks about me as if I were half god. She won't give me the gift of flaws. And this is what worries me the most, that she wants me to save her. She talks about how beautiful our love is, how wonderful it would be if we got a little house in the Valley and brought my friends and relatives up from Salvador. Any woman who talks that way a month into a relationship wants to be saved— from what, I don't know.

If I knew, I could at least offer
advice. But María doesn't want advice.
She wants a whole new self. It's too great
a burden for me. It's all I can do to keep
my own mind in one piece, far from the
knowledge that I might never return
home. How do I say these things to her?
Do I just let things continue until they
fall apart? The warmth of her flesh is all I
have to make me forget. But alcohol
does the same thing. Am I using her? Or
is she using me each time she looks at me
and loves what is not there?

—JL ROMERO

Until now, I haven't had the nerve to translate
one line from José Luis's journal. I should have
just buried it. I might have saved myself the pain
of having to open it up to identify the remains.
Before he went away he asked me to keep his
notebook because he feared the authorities could

use it against him if they found it on him and pieced together his true identity. Now, all these years later, my life has come to a halt because of words written long ago by a man whose name I didn't even know. One new testament is all it takes to warp time, to call into question the neatly bound volume of trivia and revelations you thought was your history. He was right to leave his notebook with me. It has not betrayed his identity. But it is betraying mine, handing it over to be tried before a court in which I am the jury and judge.

I said earlier that I have forgiven myself; it is not true. I look back and see a woman who was naive and sad, who looked to a refugee to save her from fear—the kind of fear that destroys, cell by cell, because it rampages undetected, unnamed. No, I haven't forgiven myself for being disappeared from myself any more than I have forgiven him. You see, there's more to the story than I have let on, more than I ever intended to let on. All these years I have told myself that he returned to El Salvador, that the authorities found him and killed him; this was what happened to most Salvadorans who got deported. But the truth is, I don't know what happened to him.

And all these years I have avoided calling José Luis by his true name, desaparecido, disappeared one. My altar should have a photograph of him, the date of his birth, and a question mark for the date of his death inscribed below his face. But I'm a coward. I couldn't bring myself to draw a question mark much less live with it day in and day out. But God was wiser. He carved that question mark into my heart and kept watch over it until I could wake up and cry out. José Luis disappeared. He defied the ordinary scheme of things in which one is either dead or alive and I cannot forgive him for this. And I cannot forgive myself for loving him now, twenty years too late, in ways I could not love him when I looked to him to swim out in the dark waters of my life and save me.

I have not laid hands on this story for six days, have not gotten near the paper. It has taken me this long to move beyond the resentment I feel at having told you the part of the story I had intended to keep to myself. Resentment, because in telling you—whoever you are—I opened the wound. I told myself the part of the story I had hoped to keep from myself, the disappeared part. But the unspoken words were turning into hooks, they were caught in my throat. Once a story is begun the whole thing must be told or it kills. If the teller does not let it out, the tale will seize her, and she will live it over and over without end, all the while believing she is doing something new. The Great Circle will come to represent not life but stagnation, repetition; she will die on a catherine wheel of her own making.

Things began to happen. There were times he didn't call, times he didn't say I love you, non-events that hurt in little ways, like paper cuts, but that added up. It could be these nonevents had happened all along, the normal ups and downs of relationships. But at a certain point, I began to perceive that he was pulling away from me and thinking about other things. And fear ate at my heart like battery acid. But it's very likely that I only imagined him pulling away, imagined the whole thing. You see, the fear I am best at is always based upon a myth. It could be that the whole time José Luis was growing closer to me. He used to clip flowers from Soledad's garden and give them to me, stems wrapped in foil, one of hundreds of small ways he showed he cared. But all these acts took place against a backdrop of flight—the assumption that to survive one sometimes must flee all that is loved. This is what terrified me. His body was branded with the equation, *love equals flight.*

Sometimes we made love in my Old Town house, the mud house that the sun baked and cracked. The thick sheets of plastic I taped over my windows for winter insulation were down and the lace tablecloth I had pinned to a curtain rod could not thwart the gaze of tourists who occasionally mistook my house for a shop. So before we made love, I took a length of golden cloth that was seared with red Farsi characters and tacked it to the wood frame above the window. I don't know what the characters meant. A man who sold lamp parts at the flea market had it among his wares; he couldn't say where it came from, but he swore it was the color of luck. The forked letters were beautiful. The sunlight that strained through them dyed my bedroom a golden yellow; I felt I was moving through flames. In the heat and light we made love like the last two animals on earth. We struck at each other with our tongues like cobras. We twisted around one another and vowed never to let go. The fear that he would one day leave me jetted through my arteries. Fear was my yoga—it loosened my limbs and elongated my breath. It opened my third eye to the myriad possibilities of misshapen mattresses on nineteenth-century floorboards.

The silence of the golden room with its blue walls and white door frames was astonishing. At most, we whispered to one another. To try to keep the room cool, we kept the door leading outside open. A sarong from Bali, the color of apricot skin and just as thin, hung over the screen; it was all that separated us from the din of tourists. Keeping quiet, we read the braille of one another's bodies. Keeping quiet, he moved on top of me, found his way in. Afterwards, he whispered, I love you. I love you, I said. I remember how those words moved up and down my thighs, how, over time, they evoked not happiness but a thrill. You see, after a certain point nothing resembling peace filled me in that room except perhaps, for the smoky, gold light. No, it was all a thrill, exactly as one might feel after parachuting from a plane, joy dependent upon fear. José Luis's body unclenched, he kissed my eyelids, my nose. He would have been happy, I'm sure, to rest. But I roused myself, roused him, and we had at it again. To this day, I'm not sure what aroused me more, sex itself or sex the symbol—emblem of a bond all the more magnificent because it would be torn asunder. I prayed he would stay but assumed he would not, assumed he would leave me for his war or for another woman. My mother's cells had fought one another, a civil war that took her from me. When I was three, a woman lured my father from home. This story is not about them, but it would be dishonest to disregard the role their ghosts played in my life, maybe still are playing; I had to make something beautiful out of abandonment. Long before José Luis left me, I was using sex to weld our bodies together into a bronze statue so magnificent I knew even if it shattered, each remnant could stand alone.

I remember how the room used to spin after we made love. It was always the same—to staunch the strange feelings of panic I got up, got dressed, turned on the classical station, and then took down the cloth with the Farsi words. What might have been a pleasant ritual turned into a series of regimented acts. I took down that beautiful cloth and folded it like a flag. I guess it was a way to make the room stop spinning, although I never would have admitted to myself that making love with José Luis was churning up something like chaos in me. Chaos that creates or destroys worlds, whichever comes first.

You see, real love is quiet as snow, without chaos, hard to write about. Perhaps that is why I haven't mentioned the man I have been seeing for a year, or maybe our love is just too new to have accrued meanings beyond pleasure. Our idea of a good time is a bed and breakfast in Northern New Mexico where he works for the state weatherproofing houses of the low-income and elderly. When he visits here every other weekend our time together is joyful, blessedly nondescript. His parents were survivors of the Holocaust. He loves life in a way peculiar to those free of reverence for authority, who can see through its claims, its need to order and crush life. When he comes over he tells stories of how he defies the state bureaucracy, weatherproofing in ways beyond those detailed in the code book, using whatever materials are at hand. In their Zen simplicity, his stories exorcise the inner authorities that say *quiet, don't tell*, that keep women like me from speaking the truth about their lives.

Photograph of my bedroom altar, Old Town: Santo Niño de Atocha, a Christ child on a throne who wears out his shoes as he wanders around each night doing good deeds; miniature Taos Pueblo incense burner; painting of Our Lady of Guadalupe from Nogales; African fertility doll, her coal-black head shaped like pita bread; mouthwash bottle filled with holy water Soledad had a priest bless; a film canister full of healing earth from the sanctuary at Chimayó. I liked it that José Luis and I made love in the presence of my santos. I knew they had blessed my love for him, however imperfect it was, however mad. They were not like the white God I'd had to kill, that women like me must kill if we are to have any hope of ever finding God. Nothing replaced Him for a long time. But looking back now I can see that the growing chaos inside blazed away dead growth, clearing a space, however violently, for God to be reborn.

There were so many moments I would rather not talk about but in this dark night of remembering, they are blooming like night flowers. I remember waiting for his phone call as I sat in the kitchen counting the tablecloth's red and white checkerboard squares. A volunteer who had taken him to meet with his lawyer had also invited him out for dinner. She was one of those women who knew everything there was to know about El Salvador, who ate and drank and slept El Salvador, who wanted to give birth to another Salvadoran. At least this is the lie that I told myself to justify my envy and fear. When no phone call came, I curled up like a shrimp until midnight cast its nets and hauled me to sleep. Another time I held my finger above the flame of my Guadalupe candle and held it there to see how long I could take the heat. When he didn't call, my world shriveled. Fetal position. Blistered finger pad. Or when he called and didn't say, I love you, I shattered, then mistook a piece of me for the whole, a mistake that disfigures women's lives time and again. But I lacked the nerve to tell him how I was feeling. When his phone calls finally came, our conversations usually went something like this: María, I would have called earlier but I ended up helping some friends translate Urgent Action Alerts after the meeting. A literacy worker in El Salvador found red crosses, the death squads' signature, painted on her walls. We started a telephone tree. Everyone is calling two friends and asking them to send telegrams to the embassy. . . . Don't apologize, José Luis. It's not that late, I was just sitting here reading the horoscopes.

URGENT ACTION ALERT

Following is a summary of KEY EVENTS in El Salvador for the month of AUGUST.
8/5 Guerrillas enter Belén north of the city and hold public meetings.
8/6 Twenty-six families occupy the abandoned Aragón hacienda in San Vicente.

8/8 Archbishop José Grande
denounces destruction of crops
by the Mixtec Battalion (trained
at the U.S. Army School of the
Americas, Fort Benning, Ga.).
8/13 Catholic Church officials
announce that the military budget
for El Salvador is likely to
increase four percent next year.
The amount used to pay the
foreign debt will increase by 400
percent.
8/20 Third anniversary of the
Santa Ana massacre.
8/25 Sixty families in villages
north of San Vicente denounce
army bombardment of their area.
8/30 Archbishop Grande
announces findings of his human
rights commission. Interviews
with surviving witnesses indicate
El Cordero was the site of an
army massacre. No estimates yet

on numbers of dead but could be close to 200. U.S. State Department officials question commission's findings and criticize American reporters who travel to the site. U.S.-trained Mixtec Battalion believed to be involved.

URGENT ACTION:

Write politely worded letters to President Alfredo Amérigo (registered mail, address on page two) asking for the release of catechist Margarita Bautista, who has been detained by Treasury police for over a month after speaking at a peace rally outside the Cathedral in San Salvador. Send copies to the White House and your representatives. See other side for updated list of disappeared and extrajudicial executions.

September 1982

1. Boil lavender in water and steam face
(lavender to harmonize body and soul)
2. Make a list of job-hunting tasks
3. Do a 20-minute *ONG NAMO
GURU DEV NAMO* meditation
4. Go visit the sick or elderly or join a
cause
5. Get out of yourself.

He hasn't called, so I'm making a
list. I'm making a list so I won't fall apart.
I won't fall apart if I follow through on
the list. If I follow through, I'll forget
about him and therefore set up the
karmic conditions that will allow him
to call.

Now I remember why, in junior
high, I used to write letters to myself
("Dear Mary") when I was feeling really
good. I sealed them away in envelopes
and opened them whenever I sank into
sadness and paralysis. They always
included pep talks, reminders of fun

times, and to-do lists. I always said to myself, "I promise this won't last forever" and I signed them, "the real you."

Now, as I write this, I can't remember the real me. It's terrifying, that you can love someone so much that you lose your own self in the uproar. I can't remember the me who loves September, who loves to walk or read. It's incredible outside. I can hear the hooves of horses pulling carriages around the plaza, San Rafael's bells, the daily "shoot-out" for the tourists in front of Wild West Saloon. I know in my mind that I would feel better if I got out. But my body can't follow through.

At times like this I wish I had hobbies or political causes. My mother used to tell me, "develop your inner resources." I should have listened. That's how she survived Dad's leaving her. That's how she survived her death. She read bestsellers, she went on retreats at

the Franciscan House, she recorded
Soledad's memories of coming up from
Mexico, she even took up folk dancing
and said, without any bitterness, that if
she'd taken it up earlier she wouldn't
have gotten cancer, but at least she
knows this for the next life. Thank God
I've at least got this notebook. As long as
I can keep moving my hand across the
page I know I won't die of depression.

Here is a photograph of me and José Luis sitting
on the adobe banco in front of San Rafael
Church, frozen in mid-laugh. Behind us roses are
growing wild around the rectory's arches. With
his Tibetan eyelids and Mayan cheekbones, José
Luis looks like a god, an obsidian idol native
people buried beneath Catholic shrines and
revered under the noses of priests. He had slipped
a rose behind my ear, a bud opening like the
mouth of a hungry infant. I have on a purple
T-shirt that I'd cut the collar out of to make it
cooler. It's slipping to the right; there's a whisper

of a black bra strap. My long hair is black with red highlights, my face olive. When a tourist snapped this photograph with my camera, my face had already taken on the full, fleeting beauty of young women the summer before something happens to make them ripen, the summer before the first fragile harvest of wisdom. The kind of beauty that returns much later in life if one can surrender all acquired wisdom and begin again.

I see now, looking at José Luis, that his face had grown too old too quickly. His face is wise but in the way that sometimes prefigures death. The lines, like those in a palm, seem to have been put there by fate, not by choice. The wonder is that his eyes, which had seen too much, are filled with laughter and forgetting. We must have just made love. The photo is proof: I could take the war out of him for a few hours, I had some power. But back then I knew nothing about the healing arts. Nobody warned me that the war left his body by way of mine, that currents of his memories were moving through me at dangerously high voltages. Look, even in this happy photograph, my eyes are hard as arrowheads. But I can't lie, can't say no one warned me. Soledad tried. I listened but refused to hear. What she said is lost on me to this day.

September 16

Maybe María is the one. Maybe my María is to be my wife. We could have children. I could begin again. We could get married in a Quaker ceremony. I could live with that. María has a problem with the Church not ordaining women, and I'm sure God agrees with her. We could raise our children as Quakers, get a place near the Meeting House in the Valley. My God, I'm starting to sound just like her. Claiming to be practical (to prevent my deportation), she weaves these fantasies. And it's getting harder and harder not to be seduced by them.

Why am I fighting her? María may abhor reality but that doesn't mean truth is not on her side. Marrying her would solve many problems. My fate would not depend entirely on a political asylum application. So far, the volunteers have worked hard to gather my documentation, sometimes even smuggling into the country taped testimony of what happened to me. But the U.S. is turning down most applications of Guatemalans and Salvadorans.

Still, the idea of marrying aside, the process of applying could buy me some time, three years maybe. With luck the authorities might misplace my file for a few more years; it has been known to happen. Meanwhile, I would have a work permit, and I could live in the light of day again. I wouldn't have to be afraid all the time. As it is, I look in the mirror and see a map of El Salvador. María's Harvard T-shirts can't cover up my skin color.

But what if in the end I apply and the U.S. turns down my application?

The government will deport me. If I try then to go underground, the authorities would have my face and fingerprints on record. To make matters worse, there are rumors that immigration routinely sends information about political asylum candidates back to El Salvador, which means if I were ever deported, it would be the end. Applying to Canada is an option, but I hear they may be tightening up their immigration policies. In truth, Canada might be as dangerous as Salvador. The loneliness, not to mention the cold, could kill me. At least here I am functioning like a human being.

So why then do I not go along with María's dreams and schemes? Am I afraid that even if we were to marry, the pull might be too great? That one night I might wake up, hear the call, and go back to El Salvador? I'm not ready to commit to another country, much less a woman. But this limbo is not doing me any good either. I know it is my destiny to go back, that it is the will of God for every Salvadoran to go back home. But right now evil is more powerful than all of us. The land problem and the civil war could easily continue for another decade. I must not assume the way will open for me to return. It is not possible to assume anything, this is the problem, this is what it means to be a refugee. Sometimes I forget I'm a refugee.

—JL ROMERO

Sweat and heat: The memory of it keeps me from getting to the sad part of the story. In the summer of 1982 a steamy Rio Grande opened the pores of the city and released aromas of mesquite, pine, and cedar. The heat made it easier for me to find those places on José Luis's body that were oblivious to the war. After we made love, I often smelled bougainvillea near the place where his heart beat like wings against the bars of a cage. And I came to understand why José Luis and others like him risked everything— even if they were too young to remember life without war, their bodies remembered; their very cells concealed the scent of a healed El Salvador. The days the temperature climbed to dizzying heights I believed in God. I believed He devised the sense of smell so that people would struggle not for abstract ideas but for memory— the scent of the land and wind before men invented war.

September 14, 1982

Mija—

    Of course I'll teach you about the old remedios. You can start by going to the co-op and buying what I've listed below, remedios from my childhood and from my guidebook. How times change. The gringos don't laugh at us anymore when we boil up our little plants.

*They're reading "the studies" about how good
all this is for you. For once science is on our
side. And now I can thank God you're
interested, if not in politics, then at least in
the old ways. (My godmothering has not been
in vain.) To start your medicine cabinet,
go get:*

- *Garlic and onions (eat them all the time,
  you should also place sliced onions on
  windowsills to kill cold germs)*
- *Ajenjibre (for hangovers)*
- *Albacar (for cramps)*
- *Cascara Sagrada (for regularity)*
- *Damiana (to raise your spirits) (it also
  acts as a stimulant in another way, but
  we won't talk about that)*
- *Jojoba oil (for beautiful skin)*
- *Manzanilla (for insomnia)*
- *Oshá (tastes like strong celery, causes you
  to break into a sweat when you chew it
  which gets cold and flu poisons out of
  you) (also said to ward off evil, in the
  old, superstitious days, they used to sew*

*it into hems of skirts to scare away
rattlesnakes)*

- *Yerba buena (for all of the above)*
- *Good supply of Laredo, Texas, miracle
candles, not to practice magic but to
concentrate the mind on the healing
powers of Our Lord*

*This will be a good start. Now
remember, food is the best medicine. All this
depression going around—it's because we've
gotten too far away from the foods of our
ancestors. And our cells never forget. Beans,
rice, avocado, cilantro, etc. We must make
every effort to eat what our elders ate, eat
with the seasons, and eat what is grown
nearby. All these new-fangled drugs aggravate
illness but hide the symptoms. No wonder
we're all crazy.*

*Now I know you wear that crystal around
your neck. If you ask me, some of that New
Age Santa Fe stuff can be as bad as drugs.
People start out trying to cure a cold and next*

thing you know, instead of taking garlic and lemon water, they've hired someone to "channel" the voice of a Visigoth. Before you go knocking on heaven's door, it's best to look for cures a little closer to home. Roots, seeds, bark, oils, flowers, etc. It says somewhere in the Bible that the earth is our cure, or something like that.

I confess I believe in reincarnation (purgatory isn't a place but a coming back again and again until we learn all our lessons). But just because you believe in past lives doesn't mean you should dabble in them. Your ancestors were Jews (before the Inquisition) in the Old World and Christians and medicine men in this one. I guess that covers your bases as good as anything. Respect your current "incarnation." I'm off on this tangent because even here in Arizona, of all places, people are getting into "channeling." Only here it doesn't cost so much. If you want my opinion, I don't see much difference between all that and what my grandma did,

*praying in tongues at the Spanish Assemblies
of God. Except it was free and anyone could
do it.*

*I tell you all this because you can't study
herbs without a sense of the ins and outs of
the spiritual life. It all works together. You
can see why I hate doctors (except our Socialist
friend who helps refugees for free). And since I
am your godmother, I want to keep you on
the straight and narrow, what with all that
New Age out there. Beware of
fundamentalists, even the ones with crystals,
hippie sandals, and trust funds. Now that's
not to disrespect true spiritual seekers. After
all, some of those Santa Feans have Free
Tibet bumper stickers on their vans. So if
turning inward helps them turn outward to do
something useful in this vale of tears, then
maybe God works even in the New Age. But
I know you're not into politics (yet, ha ha).*

Now be good. Or at least be careful.

Love & Prayers,
Soledad

One day—was it late September or early October?—Soledad returned. And she knew by the play of shadow and light on my face and in my voice that it was done: José Luis and I were lovers. She was my godmother, my mentor. She knew better than to quell the Spirit, the spirit of light that is love and the spirit of recklessness that is something else altogether. In her life, with her husbands, divorces, her breaking the rules of the church, in all these experiences and more, Soledad had seen the two faces of God. So she was not about to tell me not to live dangerously. She might offer advice to ease the blows, but she would never say, do not love him. She was a healer precisely because she had suffered and savored the faces of God, the dark and the light. And every remedio, she said, has elements of both, of the sickness and its cure. I am thirty-nine now, eleven years younger than Soledad was the summer José Luis and I were lovers, and I am just beginning to fathom what she meant.

"Mijita, be careful, when I was your age I gave my heart away, and it took me years to find it again. Mijita, my Carlos was a good man but the war made him loco sometimes, and he would leave home for days. No, no, the only way to take the war out of a man is to end the war, all wars. What do you mean, the power of positive thought? You've been reading too many of those Eastern mystical books. You can't even hear yourself think in El Salvador. I know, I've been there, it's spooky as all get out. You know, the best thing you can do is to be his friend. Now I sound exactly like my mother. And you know what? I never did a damn thing she said until I was over 40. . . ."

I wish I had written down whatever it was that Soledad told me. All I can do now is imagine her words, but it's not hard because I can see her: tobacco-colored hair, old jeans and a "Boycott General Electric" T-shirt, light brown skin prematurely creased because she loved life too much to care about the latest creams for peeling away wrinkles. In my memory, she is always chopping cilantro or heating corn tortillas on the blue flame of her gas stove. Before she quit smoking, her evening ritual consisted of holding a cigarette to the flame, sucking in a deep breath, then turning on the radio. She kept a shortwave on her windowsill next to a bottle of green dish soap. After a smoke she washed dishes, then listened to news of El Salvador tearing apart like bread. She never spoke much about the man she had married, then divorced, to keep him from being deported. At first even I was fooled; I thought she had married for love. And in a sense, she had. Having no children of her own, she adopted El Salvador. She knew its provinces, its disappearances. Every day she scanned Mexican and U.S. newspapers for news of deaths, crops, army movements, culling moments in history as carefully as she picked pebbles from beans before putting them to soak. One day she had me proofread a letter she was about to take to the post office. Dear Senator Marciando, My friends and relatives are being killed, she wrote, words short and fiery as fuses. By nature, Soledad tended away from anger. But she could pull it out and wave it like a knife when she heard of yet another death threat in the country she'd come to love.

Here is a recipe Soledad wrote out on a three-by-five card and taped to her refrigerator.

POSOLE

12:45 Wash corn (8 lbs.) several times

1:15 Put corn to boil

1:30 Corn begins to boil. Cook two hours. In separate pan put cut-up pork (7 lbs.) to boil plus $3/4$ whole onion plus 1 or 2 cloves garlic.

3:30 Put meat in with corn. If corn water is getting low, add some pork broth. Add salt & oregano. Cook about $1/2$ to 1 hour more.

Have fun!

"Mijita, your mother was right, you need to have some hobbies or sure enough, you'll develop melancolía. You'd be amazed at how learning to cook takes your mind off men—if you do it for your own pleasure. Why do you think I'm such a good cook? I was your age once, don't forget that. I know how it feels, to feel so in love that the sun and the moon trade places, it's so crazy. But be careful. No, no, I'm not saying I don't want it to work out, I do. But every woman should have a special place inside where she can think, where no man is allowed, a place that will, you know, endure. Why do you think I took up letter writing? No man is worth falling apart over. Take it from me. Now come on, let's go take a walk."

One day, Soledad's heart gave out. She had given so much to everyone but herself. When I went to the mortuary to view her body, I started to grieve all over again. Someone had cleaned her hands, wiped away the film of newsprint that had always marked them. That night at San Rafael Church, I said good-bye to her one last time before the open coffin. And pretending to touch her hand in a gesture of grief, I slipped the first few paragraphs of an Associated Press article under her palm. Two days before her death, Salvadoran guerrillas and government leaders signed an accord, shook hands all around, and proclaimed "cautious optimism" to a disbelieving world. I had cut out the article and taped it to my refrigerator next to a prayer for peace. Maybe Soledad was ready to go. Maybe she knew she had succeeded in teaching me to love a broken world.

SAN SALVADOR, El Salvador, Aug. 15, (AP)—The bodies of two nuns who were reported missing earlier this week have been found 33 miles north of

here near the village of
Encarnación.

A group of Encarnación
youth found the partially nude
bodies yesterday evening while
playing near a ditch. Authorities
have identified the remains as
those of Eve O'Connor and
María Quinto of San Antonio,
Texas.

Witnesses say the bodies,
which were in a shallow grave,
appeared to have been mutilated.
The bodies were moved to an
unrevealed location for autopsies.

The nuns were reported
missing after they failed to return
Wednesday night to their
residence, Casa Justicia, in San
Salvador.

U.S. Ambassador to El
Salvador, Emory Newland, who

oversaw the removal of the
bodies, denounced the deaths and
promised a full investigation by
an independent commission.

"Despite major steps toward
reform in El Salvador, it is clear
the country still runs the danger
of becoming a death-squad
democracy," Newland said.

But according to separate
press releases issued early this
morning by the U.S. State
Department and Salvadoran
President Alfredo Amérigo,
"leftist guerrillas" are the key
suspects in the deaths.

The differing interpretations
of the cause of the nuns' deaths is
the most recent example of a
growing rift between Newland
and the State Department,
sources said.

In recent weeks, Newland has

made widely reported visits to literacy projects, which O'Connor and Quinto helped found throughout El Salvador. The nuns belong to Our Lady of the Light, an order that has worked closely with Jesuit priests in literacy and public health.

Since the assassination last year of Jesuit Father Milton Gustavo, U.S. Jesuit leaders have alleged that the State Department is concealing evidence of a campaign by the Salvadoran army to harass church workers who live among El Salvador's poor.

Sources close to the State Department said Newland's visits to the literacy projects have embarrassed U.S. officials.

O'Connor and Quinto were outspoken critics of the $1-million-a-day in military aid the

U.S. sends to El Salvador, where
civil war has resulted in the
deaths of an estimated 50,000
people. The nuns have also
worked closely with the Mothers
of the Disappeared, a group the
Salvadoran government says has
strong ties to the guerrillas.

In his press release, President
Amérigo said he has postponed a
speech he was to give at Harvard
University's John F. Kennedy
School of Government in order
to attend the women's funeral
mass. The date of the service will
be announced soon, said a U.S.
embassy spokesman.

According to a statement
released by the San Salvador
archdiocese, Archbishop José
Grande, who has come under
repeated death threats himself,
will lead a three-mile funeral

procession from the sisters'
residence to Our Lady of Sorrows
Cathedral where he will offer a
Mass of the Resurrection.

Twenty years later, the article is brittle but the
memory is not. In the basement by the washing
machine, I am translating the *Albuquerque Herald*
report of the nuns' deaths for José Luis, and he
hates me for what happened. See, see what is
being done to us? he says. He has heard the story
of slain nuns too many times so he wads up and
throws his nation's history at me like a rough
draft. He says, you don't know what it's like to
suffer. I say, José Luis, please, it will be all right.
He says, you have no right to say that, you don't
know what it's like to flee. Later in the day, he
apologizes for the episode, but it is too late. Like
a man who dared to look straight at the sun, he
will never completely obliterate that dark light; it
has scorched his vision. He saw in me an image
of a gringa whose pale skin and tax dollars are
putting his compatriots to death. My credentials,

the fact that I am Mexican American, don't count now; in fact, they make things worse. In his anger he looks at me and sees not a woman but a beast, a Sphinx. Earlier in the morning, he had made love to a Chicana. But after telling him the news of the nuns' deaths, I am transfigured. For a terrible, disfigured moment, I am a yanqui, a murderess, a whore.

EMERGENCY ACTION BULLETIN

IN RESPONSE TO THIS WEEK'S
DEVELOPMENTS IN EL SALVADOR,
THERE WILL BE A
DEMONSTRATION AT THE
FEDERAL BUILDING DOWNTOWN,
242 WASHINGTON S.E., AT NOON.
IF YOU WOULD LIKE TO HELP
MAKE SIGNS, JOIN US AT THE
JUSTICE CENTER TWO HOURS
PRIOR TO THE DEMONSTRATION.
OTHERWISE, BRING YOUR OWN

SIGNS. KEEP THE MESSAGE CLEAR
AND SIMPLE, SUCH AS U.S. OUT OF
EL SALVADOR, BREAD NOT
BOMBS, TAX DOLLARS ARE
KILLING CHILDREN, ETC. WE WILL
ALSO BRING WHITE CROSSES
INSCRIBED WITH THE NAMES OF
SALVADORANS WHO HAVE BEEN
KILLED AND DISAPPEARED IN THE
LAST FEW MONTHS. WHEN WE
GATHER AT NOON, JOSÉ LUIS
ROMERO WILL OFFER AN
INVOCATION WITH RABBI ANNE
WEISEN. WE WILL THEN LINE UP
ALONG WASHINGTON. WE
ENCOURAGE PARTICIPANTS TO
WEAR SUITS, TIES, DRESSES, ETC.
RELIGIOUS LEADERS SHOULD
WEAR HABITS, COLLARS, AND SO
FORTH. THE MEDIA HAS MANAGED
TO PEG US AS THE RADICAL
FRINGE, AND WE NEED TO

125

COUNTER THIS STEREOTYPE IN
ORDER TO GET OUR MESSAGE
ACROSS.

THOSE WHO PLAN TO COMMIT
CIVIL DISOBEDIENCE (ONLY THOSE
WITH EXPERIENCE, PLEASE)
SHOULD MEET AT THE JUSTICE
CENTER AN HOUR BEFORE THE
DEMONSTRATION TO GO OVER
INSTRUCTIONS. WE PLAN TO
OCCUPY SENATOR MARCIANDO'S
OFFICE UNTIL HIS PEOPLE CALL
THE POLICE. WE WILL PROBABLY
BE BOOKED AND RELEASED ON
OUR OWN RECOGNIZANCE SO
PLAN FOR A LONG EVENING.
SOLEDAD SANCHEZ IS
ORGANIZING A CIVIL
DISOBEDIENCE SUPPORT GROUP,
WHICH WILL HOLD A PRAYER
VIGIL OUTSIDE THE BUILDING
UNTIL EVERYONE IS RELEASED

FROM THE POLICE STATION
ACROSS THE STREET. CALL HER
OR THE JUSTICE CENTER IF YOU
HAVE ANY QUESTIONS. PEACE.

VIGIL PROGRAM, P. 2

AFTER THE INVOCATION, PLEASE
TURN AND FACE THE FEDERAL
BUILDING AND TOGETHER READ
THE LITANY OF NAMES. THESE
ARE PEOPLE WHO HAVE
DISAPPEARED IN THE PAST
MONTH:

CARLOS RAMOS GRANDE
EUGENIA MÁRQUEZ NÚÑEZ
RUTILIO LÓPEZ MONTES
OSCAR DONOVAN MARTÍNEZ
REGINALDO DE JESÚS ROMERO
ELBA VELÁSQUEZ TAMAYO . . .

I pray that María forgives me for getting
angry with her the other day. I acted as if
it were her fault that the sisters were
killed. I suspect the real reason for my
anger is that I have no idea what to say
to make her understand that my world is
falling apart around me. And I am too
proud to say, María, there are reasons
why I get cold whenever I hear
helicopters or sirens. There are reasons
why I had to fight off vomiting last week
when we drove to Old Town and saw a
dead, bloody dog on the side of the road.
The problem is we're not seeing or
hearing the same things. Even church
bells mean something different to us. She
hears them and sets her watch. I hear
them and remember the endless funerals
in the villages outside the capital.

But what right do I have to be
angry with her? It is not her fault that her
culture has made her who she is. And

there are times when she steps out, when she sees things. Yesterday she drove me to an appointment with a counselor. I let her talk me into it because the man is a Chicano who speaks Spanish and who understands the situation of refugees. As we were walking toward the office, I spotted life-size chalk drawings of human figures on the pavement. I began to panic and I turned around and went back to the truck. I couldn't stop myself. Thank God María did not think I was changing my mind about going to the counselor. She understood what was happening. She had read in some newsletter about how the Salvadoran police outline in chalk the bodies that they find, documenting the "mysterious" deaths they themselves plan and carry out. María understood, and she sat with me in the truck until I stopped shaking. The counselor was upset when I told him what happened. He said some children had made them as part of "art therapy" with another counselor and that he would have them removed.

I have not done well since hearing the news of the sisters' deaths. I had often visited the literacy projects with Father Gustavo. Sleep has been difficult, and I find myself taking extra sleeping pills from María's purse without telling her. But I know she knows I've been drinking way too much. I feel that a bomb is ticking inside me, and I don't know how or when it will go off. It takes so little to push me off the edge. The other day, María took me to the Rio Grande for a walk. Green-gold gourds were growing wild among trees she said were Russian Olives. Just for fun, María started kicking a little gourd. After a while, for no reason at all, she smashed it with her foot. Only my pride kept me from crying. Then I was angry at her for doing what she did. In a world

of violence you would think she had
something better to do than to smash a
baby gourd.

Then I hated myself for being
angry. To make reparations, I plucked a
new gourd and tossed it in the Rio
Grande, the great jeweled snake of a river
that I have come to love. I didn't know
what else to do. It made no sense to
apologize to María so I apologized to God.

—JL ROMERO

August 22

I am working on a collection of poetry
for María, to keep my mind clear and to
give her something to remember me by
if I leave. It is tempting to save them
until that day comes, if it comes. If I give
them to her now, she will take it to
mean I am in love with her. And I do
love her. But she might miss the larger
meaning, that I never know where I will
be tomorrow. I want to give her what I

can now, but not foster hopes of a
future. In truth, the situation is not fair. I
talk with her about the importance of
hope while praying she will not dare
dream.

#3 FOR MARÍA

how your eyes hold me,
eyes where relief and fear
reside as in a cease-fire.
my rib throbs beneath
your palm, the rib
they fractured with
a rifle, the rib
that if taken into
the body of america
might make it new,
a country where mercy
and nobility reside,
where the shattered
bones of my people

teach your people
about strength.
    —JL ROMERO

One day he told me about the strange markings
on his hands and his back. Sitting on the end of
the bed, he sucked on a cigarette and flicked
ashes in a beer can that he held between his
thighs. He said, guards snuffed out their cigarettes
on my body, one by one. It says so in the affidavit, thirty-three burn marks, not birthmarks
like I told you the first time we made love. As he
spoke his face melted into a trail of waxy tears,
but because he believed men should never cry, I
looked the other way. Not only cigarettes, he
said, but electric wires on my genitals. Then, as if
I were a stranger whom he had run out of things
to say to at a party, he turned away, tapped his
finger on the beer can. He felt ashamed. Not
because he survived while others died but

because the intimacy was too much, a window thrown open too wide. To tell another person about what was done to your body in the name of politics is a frightful act of intimacy, risky beyond sex, because a man can make love for years and not reveal much of himself at all.

I took the almond oil, offered to rub his back, his shoulder blades that tensed like birds' wings before flight. Beneath my hands was a constellation of markings that in any other life-time might have been a momentary flushing of skin in the fire of passion, marks left by a woman's fingernails. And as I so often did in those days, I refused to believe my own eyes. I refused to believe that what I was seeing was a pattern of scars, the legend to the map of his life—1982, someone had branded those numbers into his back. You had to really look to see, as if searching heaven for the big dipper on a cloudy night. Nineteen eighty-two was the year he was tortured, that thousands were tortured. In a country the size of Massachusetts. In a country named after Christ.

Later, as I massaged his temples, his eyes turned to glass—rearview mirrors that let him look back many miles, many months, at a woman I sensed had touched him just as I was doing. A woman I feared had met the same fate as the nuns, their bodies not merely "mutilated" as the newspapers reported, but their hands cut off as a warning to all who would dare try nursing a nation back to health.

A few weeks after the nuns' deaths, I found a poem in Spanish folded in José Luis's Bible. I put it back after reading it, pretended it was not there, told myself I hadn't seen it, and so assured that its shape would be preserved in my memory forever, like autumn leaves ironed between sheets of waxed paper.

LAMENTATION

When at last my man
gets out
to become a new man
in North America,

when he finds a woman
to take the war out of him,
she will make love to a man
and a monster,
she will rise
from her bed,
grenades
ticking in her.

The poem was signed, "Ana."

Three

My son, José Luis, is nineteen years old. On his breaks from college in New York City he always comes home—to a brown mushroom of a house that seems to have sprung from the fertile mud of the Valley, the house that Soledad coated with mud and straw before her death, before she signed it over to me. After meeting José Luis yesterday at the America West gate, I helped lug his knapsacks and other bundles, embarrassed at my secret joy in knowing he still brings jeans and sweatshirts home to be washed. It is all part of the myth we share, the pact—he lets me do his laundry and indulge in some semblance of mothering, some illusion of authority. Like all children, he had to have sensed his mother's grief over the nature of things: that a child, sprouted like a plant from a clipping of one's own flesh, grows up and away, becomes a person unto himself. Feeling my loss when he went away to college, he hit upon the ritual of the unwashed clothes; he also lets me call him mijito, my little boy. And in return I try to refrain from telling him what to do with his life, his world.

Oftentimes, after supper, when I would rather we go on a walk, José Luis descends to the basement where, years ago, we set up his first computer. Messages flash like lightning on the screen and he answers, communicating for hours at a sitting with students in Brazil, biologists in China—wherever wetlands or highlands or any other land is in danger of disappearing, of becoming something it is not due to man-made chemicals that have infiltrated once pristine places. My son doesn't hear me or see me when he is clacking away at the computer. This reminds me of how he used to sit at Soledad's piano for hours and pluck out "songs." As a boy, he was drawn to the minor chords. And even now, on vacation, he prefers to be present, if only by way of computer, at a catastrophe.

How different his universe is from the one Soledad knew. José Luis and his friends cast bottles upon oceans of computer screens, and, in an instant, their messages wash up as far away as Africa. Before history happens—a land takeover, a nuclear waste accident, the death of another species—José Luis knows about it. His is a generation of psychics, not because they can peer into the future but because the sins of earlier generations have forced them to look deeply into the here and now and thereby alter fate. It is a frightful balancing act, attending to the moment in order to create the future. His basement walls are papered with maps of frayed ozone layer, dying forests, dust bowls where crops once thrived. The maps tell the real story of how the world has changed since Soledad was his age. José Luis is caught up in a struggle larger than that of an individual nation. He and his friends talk about saving the planet. I wish I could say they were exaggerating.

During his vacations we indulge in other rituals besides joking about his unwashed clothes. My favorite is where I say, mijito, how's your Spanish coming along? Just fifteen minutes a day reading the Juárez newspapers and you'll have it down, or better yet, go to the Spanish mass. . . . Then, with a grin, he asks me if I kept my part of the bargain, if I have learned to at least pronounce names of chemicals he is studying in his environmental biology class. Chemicals that my son, the budding topsoil expert, says act on the earth like cancer—cells that don't know what they are in relation to the whole.

That he and I can go back and forth this way is a sign of healing. When José Luis was in high school, I made an error I feared was fatal. I told

142

him that if he passed his Spanish class, I would send him to El Salvador for a summer, to volunteer in one of the new communities, Ciudad Grande. No sooner had the thought escaped from my mouth when a terrible storm gathered in that Olmec Indian face of his, wide and round and brown as cinnamon. He thundered: Ma, I don't wanna go there, I don't wanna major in Spanish. How come you never say anything about how good I'm doing in science? How come you never ask about my project for the Science Fair?

My son, as all children must do, indicted me on charges of conspiring to control him. He presented the evidence. And he grew up. Right there, one terrible afternoon, my baby grew up and became himself: Olmec with a warrior's helmet, raging against me and the powers that had laid waste his Earth.

When José Luis slipped into the world three months too soon, he had a fig for a face, a body no longer than a woman's size eight shoe. I had no idea how to hold a thing that small without breaking it, but it didn't matter. Nurses washed the muds off him and whisked him away to an incubator where he meowed under harsh lights, tubes, and antennae. They kept him there until his lungs showed signs of inflating, sails strong enough to catch the wind and propel him through life.

For what seemed an eternity that hospital was my home—the university hospital serving the uninsured, where a Jewish friend of Soledad's treated refugees, afterwards walking them through underground hallways and out a back door, bypassing official forms and sliding fee scales. It was there, in a room of glass mangers, that Soledad brought me food and headlines from the outside world. In the early evenings we dipped corn tortillas in thermoses filled with black beans and then went to a waiting room to listen to news from Central America on the shortwave radio. It bothered her that the doctors would not allow the radio in the "preemie" ward. Soledad wanted José

Luis from the very start to breathe the atmosphere of El Salvador, its tropical airs that she said must have had something to do with the people's ability to live for so long on so little. After the news I usually fell asleep on a rocker next to José Luis's incubator. One night as I was sleeping, Soledad taped holy cards to José Luis's glass cocoon. Mary, Joseph, St. Jude, Rafael the Archangel, a kind of ad hoc committee of divine intervention. Another night she draped an oxygen tent with rosaries blessed in Lourdes. In a crisis, Soledad had a hard time not turning blank surfaces into altars. She was all for hedging her bets, or, at the very least, somehow sanctifying the most hopeless of situations, the fruits of which she promised would be visible "if not in this life, then in the next one."

It was there, at the hospital, that I learned to proofread. I scrutinized every line on my child's face, certain that at any moment he might be a comma or period away from oblivion. A glove-like device fastened to the incubator allowed me to slip my hand in and gently poke him; the smallest stirrings restored me to peace. His eyes were shut as tightly as a new kitten's. He was all animal, a bundle of hungers. He was still in the garden and my face was a passing cloud in his sky. The news from El Salvador was a babbling brook. Looking at him, I wondered, what will I do if he leaves me, how will I live if he dies? I hated my helplessness. After months of eating the right foods and reading the right books on pregnancy and parenting, there was now not a thing I could do—except keep watch at this mystery.

Years before, Soledad told me that her great-aunt, who was of Nahuatl Indian descent, believed that it took five years for a child's body and spirit to decide whether or not to remain together. Remembering her words, I asked myself, who am I to demand that my son's flesh and breath stay together for my sake? José Luis's father taught me love could not be used like a cage to make a man stay. What if the universe now was telling me that it might take even greater love to let someone go? But I was not capable of detachment. The dream that my child would live was a rope I tied around my waist to keep me from slipping into a pit of despair. In my desperation I pleaded with God, cried out in the hope that one day He would hear the echo: let José Luis live and I will tell him the story of how he came into this world.

One night, sensing that the darkness had become too much for me, Soledad said very gently, Offer it up, mija. Offer up your pain for the mothers whose children are disappeared. There were times when I had hated Soledad's fatalism, her "si Dios quiere," her God-willings, the way, in the name of realism, she could suddenly dismantle her expectations rather than reinforce them, come what may. I did not yet understand that by accepting things as they were, Soledad found energy to try and change the world, or at least her portion of it. But that particular night, too exhausted to revert to logic and having nothing better to do, I did as she said; I offered up my helplessness, all that was small and weak and frightened inside me, on behalf of those who were worse off. And somehow, Soledad's mandate became an umbilical cord through which I received nutrients of meaning. These kept me going until doctors declared that José Luis's lungs had grown strong enough to contain his cries so that we could take him home. Since that time I have tried to interpret "offering it up" for my friends. "Empathy" does not quite embody its spirit. No, the word I think comes closest is "solidarity," and it is that word that resonates the most with my friends and my son, the nonbelievers.

By demanding that I attend a troubled entry into the world and, later, soccer games, science fairs, and graduation—by demanding not perfection but presence—José Luis drove me to ordinariness; that has been his great gift to me. He began by giving me reason to get up each morning. So that we could live, I got a job as a copy editor at the *Albuquerque Herald*. I joined a day care cooperative that the Quakers sponsored at the Meeting House. When José Luis started first grade, I signed on with the PTA and, eventually, a "Parents for Peace" project. We aimed to educate other parents about the menace of nuclear war and nuclear waste. When the elementary school principal tried to ban us from open house night, I circulated a petition demanding that we be allowed to display our literature. I presented it at a school board meeting and our request was granted. There was nothing mysterious about my budding interest in politics, which Soledad had long predicted. I wanted a better world for my son. God only knows if I have made any difference at all. But at the very least, life began to taste good to me; it became memorable. With each vote I cast or letter to the editor that I ghosted for friends, another part of me woke up.

Now, as I tell you these things, José Luis is at his computer in the basement, the room where he was conceived. The room where his father told me, I'm leaving now, I'm going back to El Salvador. Someday I have to tell my son the story of his room and the spirits that dwell there. But first, I must tell myself the rest of the story, chew on it like oshá root, sweat it out. What I can't remember, I will invent, offer up my tales for those who were not granted time enough to recall, to mend. My son is cursed with a mother who makes up stories, a liar, blessed with a mother who is a storyteller given a blank notebook and a free hour. There are some memories I would rather fight to the death. Fight, rather than say to my son, mijito, once upon a time I gave you the name José Luis in order to make it real, to make a made-up name real.

Four

That night the rain sounded like piñón nuts trickling into a mason jar.

The world smelled like wet adobe, like chamomile flowers steaming on the stove.

Black lace clouds covered the face of the full moon, then lifted. Moonlight clear as white wine emptied into the room.

I tell you all this so that you will know the night was beautiful despite . . .

A blow to the face is the color of blueberries . . .

Let me backtrack. Let me try again. Son. Mijito.

It was the last day of October. And just as a woman's cycle can get off track, the season mistook the sun for the moon or the moon for the sun and a rain that smelled like spring flooded ditches and arroyos. The rain beat down on Soledad's house, made her screen doors swell and stick. José Luis and I opened windows and talked of wanting to turn the soil, plant seeds, make things grow. We were giddy that night, your father and I, laughing at nothing at all. Without giving me any reason, he insisted I drive him to the discount store; I did, and he bought a tape player for me—they used to call them boom boxes—with money he had saved up from washing dishes. Long and squat, it had speakers on each end and knobs in the middle for tuning treble and bass. We took it down to the basement along with a six-pack of beer and put it on the chest of drawers where your father kept his

Bible and poems. During the summer he had introduced me to the music he loved: the Chileans, Víctor Jara and Violeta Parra, the exiled Salvadoran group, Yolocamba Ita, tapes he dug up from Soledad's cedar chest. These were songs of struggle, not just about love's struggles, and they began to break my heart. And as it is at times with bones, my heart needed to be broken and reset properly so it could carry me through life.

But on the night I am telling you about I wanted to hear Aretha. José Luis read my mind. He was so proud of that tape player, so proud that he could buy me a gift. He had the smile of a man about to win a marathon when he dashed upstairs to get my tape. He watched me while I put the tape in and fine-tuned the Queen of Soul. We wrapped ourselves in the starry night of her voice. Then, like pagans welcoming spring, we began to dance. I don't know what got into us but whatever it was, I've seen it in you, mijo, when spring appears for a day in February and you walk outside in shorts. I was wearing your dad's T-shirt over a white cotton skirt. My hair, which was very long, was tied back in a braid. I wore three or four rings, long black bead earrings, a diamond stud pierced in my upper right lobe. Can you believe your mother dressed like that? You must wonder why I can remember clothes in such detail. It helps me to remember feelings, that's why. And if I can describe the feelings of that night, the silk and barbed wire of it, then I will have told you the whole truth.

You see those marks under the brass handle of your top drawer? That was where we snapped open beer bottles before we sat on the bed and toasted El Salvador. Your father was as dark as you, very handsome. He had found extra work tarring roofs; the autumn sun got under his skin and stayed there. He wore patched jeans, no shirt, a St. Jude medal on a chain around his neck. He took my breath away; I'm not embarrassed to tell you this. He leaned up against the headboard, smiled for no reason. His face did not flicker with a thousand emotions like yours does; it was an event when he smiled. We held hands, watched the moon disappear behind clouds, then reappear in the basement window. The lace curtain you used to think was so "girlish" was parted; I had hung it to soften the wrought iron bars that protected the glass. For some reason José Luis got it into his head to teach me how to blow on the lip of the beer bottle, to create the sound of wood flutes he said were played in the Andes. What I'm trying to tell you is that we were happy that night, happy. Yet the word is too homely to describe what we felt.

We opened more beers; empty bottles collected beside the Sacred Heart candle on the night table. José Luis said, mornings smell like this in Salvador, like soaked earth. He said, someday I'll take you there, you would love the mornings. Your father had never said anything like this before. It was beautiful, outrageous, and we knew it would come to pass. We laughed, peaceful as oracles who know precisely how things will turn out and so are free to leave the logistics to God. José Luis may have said other things, I don't remember. But slowly, silence had its way with us. You'll see how it is someday when you fall in love. For several weeks our love had been quiet as circles radiating outward in a pond. We had forgotten the sound of the stone that started it all.

You see, your father had become my friend. No, I didn't know his real name, but he had ceased to be a stranger. The drives to Old Town, washing the floor, cleaning beans. The most mundane tasks made us real to one another. You'll know what I mean if you ever marry and stay in love. And so that night we loved one another, simply. There were no exploding stars, no insatiable hungers. We embraced with our whole bodies; we were like two hands clasped in a prayer of gratitude to the universe. Mijito, this is the night you were conceived. You were loved into being by a woman and man who, despite all the world can do to people, set aside their fears long enough to wonder at spring rain in October.

You need to know all this because I don't want you to be frightened by what happened

next. We got up and put on sweatshirts because the air had begun to thin. The window was cracked open and José Luis closed it, turned the tape over. He turned around and looked at me; it was my favorite song. Something about how you're the only thing in the world that I need, that I'll ever need. Standing there below the window, crossed with bars of shadow and light, José Luis was handsome as a god. I watched him, wanted him all over again. At that moment, I don't know why, I remembered an invitation we had received in the mail the day before. I said, we've been invited over for supper by one of the Quakers. I know you remember her. She translated for you once. Her name's Ana. . . . I never finished the sentence. In a frightening flash of movement, José Luis flattened his body against the wall as if someone around a corner were taking aim at him with a gun. He slid down to a squat. His eyes squinted into blades. I said, José Luis? But it was too late. He could no longer hear me with human ears.

Ribs heaving, he came at me like a jaguar.

And he let loose a terrible cry of *no*. Words surfaced on the dark waters of that *no*: *I've been looking for you. We found Ana's body in the ravine near the airport. I saw what you did to her hands and her tongue. You hunted her down like an animal. We were going to get married. All we wanted was an ordinary life.* I sat, paralyzed on the dark bed. For a terrible, eternal instant clouds extinguished the moonlight and my face had disappeared and become the face of the soldier who killed Ana, the soldier with no heart, dismembered and dismembering. I opened my mouth to ask, who's Ana? but nothing came out because José Luis's hands turned into fists, one for each friend whose life had been torn like a page out of history. I thought I heard the air crack, branches breaking. I guess I lifted my hands to protect myself, surely I shouted. But I'm not sure, not sure at all. Because somehow I managed to leave my body, to float away from the basement bedroom and the hammer of fists on flesh.

Seconds as long as a train's whistle passed, one by one. Then everything stopped. His hand was raised to strike me again but an invisible wire held it up, a puppet's hand. On the wall behind him his shadow stuck to peeling paint exactly like those shadows of human figures in Hiroshima, signatures left by the bomb just before flesh evaporated. His whole body had come to a halt except for his eyes. And in his eyes I could see people running and dropping, flames and plumes of smoke, processions of women holding photographs of their children, telephone poles falling, bridges flying to pieces. I'm telling you the truth, I saw all this and more in his eyes. Your father and his friends had handed their lives over to the cause of stopping the war and in the end, they could not even flee from it. All these years I have been too afraid to tell you what happened to us that night. War is a god that feasts on body parts. It deforms everything it touches, even love. It got to me, too. It cut out my tongue.

Every story has its medicine; you must figure out what you most need from this one so you can take it and let go of the rest. Maybe you will come away from what I have told you with peace. It's not your fault that anger sometimes splits you in pieces that crash like plates of earth. Those sounds penetrated my body the night we conceived you, and the blows figure into your destiny as surely as the positions of planets that ruled the night. I forgive you your rage, the rage of your teenage years that, aimed at an absent father, struck me instead. Now, son, forgive yourself.

And here, perhaps, is more medicine. I worry for you when your eyes turn to blades as you watch the news or when you pound computer keys like a wartime reporter as you write term papers about toxins and topsoil. What burdens you carry trying to save the world! It is a habit of Americans to think heaven gave us a unique destiny, that we are to spread truth among nations. Luck and too much wealth allow us to imagine ourselves in this strange light, luck and wealth that have benefited both of us. We have had the luxury, unthinkable to most people, of developing talents. Use them, José Luis. Hold to the dream of saving the world. But be at peace: you are not unique. It may be God is asking nothing of you except to remember who you are—one of millions conceived in love and war, in a night that shattered like a beer bottle on a curb as a voice called out stop, stop.

I'm tired, frightfully tired. Like snake venom, this story's medicine had to be drawn from my own body. Maybe you won't even read this, I don't know. Long ago I began this tale for reasons I could not yet articulate, maybe for no reason at all. I could not have guessed I would end up fulfilling my half of a bargain I struck with God when you were born, that if you lived I would tell you the story of your origins. Promesas are as dangerous as skydiving, leaps into thin air. Nothing frightens me more than an answered prayer. And nothing taxes a body more than giving something back to God. This is why I am so tired, why I have spent this day crying in my room. This is how badly I wanted you to live.

What happened next was almost anticlimactic, like a building caving in a few minutes after an earthquake. I was on the floor by the bed, my face wet, my body still rumbling in an endless tremor. José Luis dropped down beside me, took my hands and whispered, what have I done? I said, it's me, María. It's me, María. He looked into my eyes; he saw me cowering inside. Then we reached for one another, held on for dear life. We were like two airline passengers who are perfect strangers until the pilot announces an emergency landing. We held each other, we landed, but instead of rejoicing, we wept. I touched my cheekbone. It was a large, hot pulse. I could feel my heart pumping extra blood to put out the fire in my face. The room began to spin, sickness washed over my abdomen. Then, I remembered.

A man, a neighbor, offers to stay with me while my mother goes to the hospital to see her father, who is dying. I'm seven years old. My mother's long brown-red hair is pulled back in a braid. She kisses me. Says, I'll be back soon. The car crunches gravel as she drives away.

The man, who has just come from work, wears a tie and a suit. When he smiles there isn't really a smile there; it's a minus sign.

He says, your dress is crooked. What a pretty red dress. Let me straighten it out. But I hear, I'm going to straighten you out.

Something about the hem of my pretty dress being too short. Something about hands crawling up my thighs, thumbs under panties.

A finger in a place you hardly know exists is a knife. A knife in a place for which you have no word is the most lethal of weapons. It carves words on your inner walls to fill the void. Words like *chaos*, *slut*, *don't tell*, *your fault*.

The girl with the ponytail opens her mouth but someone has cut the wires that link thought and expression. She is receiving millions of signals, children everywhere crying out, but the speakers have broken down.

The girl is alone in the house, alone with

the man. Within minutes she learns that bad things happen when you are alone. She learns fear of being alone long before she learns to say *abandonment*.

The place of pleasure becomes the place of fear.

I can only speak of this a few sentences at a time. Bear with me. I cannot recall everything. I might never recall everything. But see the blank spaces between sentences? I promise to fill them in if I do remember. For now let the blank spaces honor that in me which is too injured to re-member. Bear with us, the thirty-nine-year-old woman, the seven-year-old girl. Honor.

The man smiles his minus sign smile, can-celing the girl. He gets up off his knees and turns on the TV. Time for the news. Men in baggy clothes that make them look like rocks or trees genuflect, set rifles on their knees, take aim. Helicopter blades shred the sky. Winds beat the jungle down from three dimensions to one. The men with guns have on helmets that look like turtles. They point their guns at small men with

almond eyes and matchstick cheekbones who come out of the trees with hands behind their heads. Smoke billows, breaks up into characters, a language that has yet to be invented. A village is burning. The village becomes a smoke signal that not even God can decipher.

The man with the tie greets the girl's mother. She has come home from the hospital; her father is not doing well. She smiles through the worry, thanks the neighbor for staying with her daughter. The man turns off the television. Says, the war will get worse before it gets better. Or was it, the weather will get worse before it gets warmer? The girl's mother gives him cookies wrapped in tinfoil. Thank you, good-bye. Thank you, good-bye. He smiles, canceling the two of them. He is dead in the eyes. The world is flat to him. He will go out and cancel whole populations.

The girl opens her mouth to say something to her mother. But she has no words for what has happened, no words for evil. Besides, it's beginning to snow, a spring snow. She presses her nose to the windowpane. Fat flakes splat on glass, stick to rocks like moss. She imagines a wonderland as white as in fairy tales her mother reads to her each night. The girl is beginning to drift off, to forget. For many years she will not know that much of what she is doing is fighting sleep.

Twenty years later I still go by the name María. When I said to José Luis, it's me, María, I remembered. And the ghost of the man with the minus sign smile fled. The demon could not bear it. He could not bear the sound of my true name.

November 2, 1982

Mijita—

    Thank heavens you called me. You've been so quiet all summer, and I was worried about you when I took off last week. I'm just grateful you know I'm here for you all the time even when I'm away. Your bruises will clear up soon enough. It's the inner bruises I worry about most. You're very wise to go to José Luis's counselor. He's a good man. It's not easy but you're on your way. The worst thing is not remembering. That's the devil's tool. As I told you, it happened to me too. I was about five. So you're not alone. I'm beginning to believe all those ladies who carry on about "the patriarchy."

You and José Luis just keep holding each other and talking to each other. Dr. You-Know-Who from the university hospital called me and reassured me the two of you will be fine. He said José Luis is responding well to the antipanic pill. It's a mild one but make sure he takes it with food. This war syndrome thing is very complicated. It's turning up more and more in our work. My contact in Nogales said that some Toronto doctors have started up a center for torture victims. I'm writing a letter to see if we can't get one of the doctors to come down and tell us about the work. If we can train some counselors and M.D.'s in some of those therapies we'll save all sorts of grief. Dr.

You-Know-Who has long said the same thing, and he should know, his parents were survivors of the concentration camps. Food, shelter, and political asylum applications have been our first priorities, but they're not enough when the weight of the past hits the fan.

On the phone last night you kept saying that you should have listened to me. Yes, I did try to warn you that something could go wrong. But neither of us can predict the future. Life is a risky business but the alternative is to dig a hole and bury yourself. You may not know it, but I have my share of scars. And I would have them even if I had never come out of the house. Better to have scars from living than from hiding. So don't beat yourself up, mijita, you've got enough bruises as it is. I'm sure there are lessons to be learned from the experience, but you can sort them out later, okay? Call me soon and fill me in on everything. I'm here for you.

Love & Prayers,
Soledad

November 1982

Someday I'll write down everything that
happened the other night. It's too
overwhelming right now. I don't know
how to begin to describe everything. But
I think I'm starting to understand why
fear and sadness have always been too
close, like my own shadow. I was hurt
badly once upon a time. And now I
know how I was hurt. There's not much
I can do with the information per se. But
maybe that's the point. What I know is
more than information. It's truth. I might
never completely "recover." But I feel I
have a chance to be free.

I've been in a stupor for like two
days, moving in and out of sleep. And
after all this time, José Luis is sleeping
very deeply. I don't dare tell Soledad he
quit taking the antianxiety pill Dr.
Weisel gave him. José Luis said he
needed to get old poisons out of him,
and so he has been chewing on oshá

root. He has let himself cry and cry, finally, about Ana, the woman he was going to marry, and about all his friends. He says that's why he's able to sleep. That tears that aren't allowed to flow poison the blood.

It's good that I know what I know because it helps me be more compassionate toward José Luis. I think a part of me envied him. It's a terrible thing to admit. When he gets up to talk in packed churches, his wounds are deep as the Grand Canyon, open to everyone. Mine have always been invisible. I mean it's not like I can stand up in front of a crowd and talk about something as dumb as sadness or fear of being abandoned or life spinning out of control. It's not on the same scale as death squads and disappearances or rich people owning all the land. But the issue isn't who got hurt more. I keep feeling like it's all part of the same pattern. Of people loving

power, or some such thing, more than
life. Who knows. Anyway, it's good that
I've got this notebook. I feel better
already, just writing things down.

I can hear you clacking away at the computer. It
makes me feel old-fashioned, writing everything
out by hand. But these years of getting up early
to scribble in my notebook have made me a crea-
ture of habit. I know of no joy as great, while
waiting for the caffeine to strike, as moving a
pen across a page. It's like watching a pointer
skirting across a Ouija board; letter by letter,
answers come. I'll admit revenge may be the root
of my joy. You see, before our neighbor moved
away, he brought my mother a cigar box filled
with pens and notebooks he said he didn't need
anymore. My mother gave them to me to practice my penmanship. She cleared a space on the
kitchen table and set up a lamp. The man who
tried to gut me like a fish had no idea what he
had done by giving away those things. I swam
and then I soared as I made up stories in note-

books that were blank except for a few pages of mathematical formulas. I like to think I am above revenge, but just imagine how sweet it feels; I got in the last word. Is this revenge? Or is it, as Soledad would surely say, the spirit working in mysterious ways?

Five

It's just amazing. I can't believe my mom and I are about to land in San Salvador. The plane is shaking like hell. We've run into interference, as the pilot keeps saying over and over, and I feel sicker than a dog. I know I shouldn't try to read now, but Mom remembered this poem she had in her purse that she says my father left her. It's by someone named Claribel Alegría. My father underlined parts of it: Return obsesses me / faces fly by / through the open fissure. / Once more there'll be peace / but of a different kind. / The rainbow glimmers / tugs at me / forcefully / not that inert peace / of lifeless eyes / it will be a rebellious / contagious peace / a peace that opens furrows / and aims at the stars. . . . Shit, I can't read anymore, I guess I'm just too nervous, but I don't dare say anything to Mom. It was my big idea to come here. After she told me all about my father, I said we have to try and find out if he's dead or alive. Even though the peace accords were signed ages ago, the San Salvador archdiocese is still trying to figure what happened to everyone; they keep all the photographs of the dead and disappeared under lock and key. I read in the newspaper that Salvadoran church leaders and members of the World Council of Churches are going before the UN to demand the opening of the mass graves. It sounds like they won't rest until everyone is accounted for. I don't know what we'll find in the archdiocese's office. It scares me to think they might have a photograph of my father's body. I've seen him in photographs, alive and smiling, and I can't imagine how it will feel to see him any other way. But mostly I'm worried for Mom.

Our flight was delayed—we didn't arrive until 1 A.M.—but Sister Margarita Bautista was there to meet us. She seemed so happy to see us. You'd have thought we were old friends. Mom says she knew Soledad, that they'd met when Soledad went on her first delegation to El Salvador. We were supposed to spend the night at Ciudad Grande, where she runs a literacy project, but it was too late to drive out there so we ended up at the Sheraton. I didn't sleep at all and neither did Mom. We stayed up for the rest of the night and played cards and she reminisced about my father. She laughed a lot remembering how he tried to teach her to make pupusas— corn pockets stuffed with cheese—and how hers always came out hard, like cookies. Then, out of the blue, Mom started crying, saying she never wrote down the recipe. I didn't know what to say, so I said, that's neat that Dad liked to cook.

All of a sudden she stopped crying. I'd never, ever called my father "Dad." But the word fit. It fit like a good pair of shoes. I think deep down inside I've always been angry at not having had a father. But after Mom told me I got my angry streak from the night he hit her, a part of me quit being angry. It never dawned on me that even though he went away, he left me parts of himself. Mom didn't just make me from scratch.

I'm scared shitless. Sister Margarita is supposed to be here any second to take us to the archdiocese office. Mom's touching up her lipstick. She always does that when she's nervous. Now she's complaining about the lone wrinkle between her eyebrows. She's paranoid about turning forty. Maybe all this is just midlife crisis. But then Mom's always been old for her age. From what she told me, it sounds like she felt too many things at too young an age. On the one hand, if I spot a gray hair she makes me pluck it. On the other hand, she says she can't wait to become the age she has always been inside—fifty. She says she might join the Peace Corps when that day comes. I can't figure Mom—oh my God, Sister Margarita is here.

The archdiocese office is not at all what I expected. It was rebuilt with cinder blocks after it was blown up—that was the same bomb that took out part of a cathedral wall and killed Archbishop José Grande, who Mom says was very famous for the stands he took on behalf of human rights. There's nothing on the walls but a cross and a picture of Jesus risen from the dead, which seems to have bullet holes in it. Sister Margarita has gone back to the safe with the sister who works here. It's crazy. They still have to keep all the documents in a safe—all these years after the signing of the peace accords. Mom is holding on to her shawl like it's about to fly away. I wish I could make her feel better. At least we're not alone. There are two other mothers here, both with children. Their heads are covered with scarves. I've never seen such faces. Tree bark faces, dark and lined, old before their time but strong. What's weird is that if you take away the lines, they look like me—the cheekbones, the Indian eyes. For all I know they could be relatives. I think Mom is thinking the same thing. One of the children fell as he walked toward us and Mom jumped out of her chair and picked him up, then pulled some tissue from her purse to wipe the kid's face as he sobbed. Now the Salvadoran ladies are talking to Mom. I wish I could understand what they were saying. Mom's going to faint when she hears I signed up for a Spanish class next semester.

For two hours we've been searching through albums and albums of photographs. I don't know why we're not running out of the room crying. You just have to go numb sometimes. You have to look at the bodies as if you were watching television. But it's not that easy because I have to search those faces for the face of my father. For my face. A couple of times Mom got up and left the room. I've never seen her look so old. In two hours she's taken on some of the features of the other women here. Her face isn't sagging like a

North American face. It's growing thinner and tighter, as if to make room for—for all the dead. It's like they take up so much space—their faces, their memories, the things they could never say. When we started going through the albums I wanted to run, to get the hell out of here. But curiosity is my strongest emotion, stronger even than fear. I want to find my father, my dad.

Mom, look, Mom, Mom, don't cry, it's okay, it's him! It's Dad. No, he's not dead. There's a question mark below the photo. See, there's his birthday but no death day. He's like he was in your pictures. Maybe he never even came back here. But look Ma, look at his name. It's José Luis Alegría. José Luis. It's not a made-up name after all! What do you mean, you knew it all along? It's okay, Mom, go ahead and cry. Don't worry about me, I'll cry later. What do you mean, you're crying with happiness? Yeah, you're right, he wasn't a stranger. See, Mom, he told you his real name because he loved you and he wanted to give you something real. I know because it sounds like something I would do. Me and Dad are funny that way, we're stubborn. Ma, you never gave me a real middle name. I've got one now. Alegría. Happiness.

The nuns are stroking Mom's back and the two other ladies who were flipping through the books are holding her hands. And all I can think about is my middle name. I should be crying. But why? Dad was always disappeared to me. But now he's come back and given me another name. And I have a strange feeling he's alive. For twenty years Mom has believed the worst. She's funny that way, we're really different. I'm convinced he's—Jesus, there's the archbishop. Sister Margarita is introducing him to Mom. It's José Grande's replacement. You'd never guess he's an archbishop because he's wearing cotton pants and a simple shirt and torn up sandals. Last year Mom sent me an article about a speech he gave at Harvard, something about how there will be no peace until all of El Salvador's dead are named and honored, and all the killers brought to justice. Now he's handing something to Mom—it's a poster. A poster of a dark lady wearing a white scarf and holding a crown of thorns. Behind her is what looks like a human figure outlined in chalk on pavement. At the bottom of the poster are the words, madre de los desaparecidos, Mother of the Disappeared. I've never seen anything like it. It's Mary the mother of Jesus.

The first thing Mom had me do when we got back was develop my film—she had me take photos of the picture of Dad. She has seemed very peaceful since we got back last week, which is good because I was worried sick that our experience would set her way back. We still don't know what the hell happened to Dad. But she seems to have a lot of energy. She's even gotten involved over at the Justice Center. She told me that at a meeting last night she volunteered to organize a letter-writing campaign—there's a push now to get a team of forensic experts to Salvador to analyze what's in the mass graves, to document just how bad things were during the war. This morning she dragged me to mass at San Rafael, and afterwards we stopped by the frame shop. When we got home, she had me put a nail in the wall above her bedroom altar and we hung the poster—she calls it an icon—of the Mother of the Disappeared. Then, she got a photograph of herself when she was seven and the photo of the picture of Dad and she stuck them in the bottom corners of the frame. She lit a candle and sat quietly for a long, long time. She didn't say a word about why she hung the poster, which is weird because she's always running around trying to analyze things, to put things in words. It drives me crazy. But finally I couldn't stand it anymore, and I asked her what she was thinking. She smiled and said that the Mother of the Disappeared is forever remembering, forever waiting for everyone to return. "Mijo, I can get on with my life now," she said.

I just finished a long conversation with my son. It's happening so quickly; in the shadow of his

lush and amber waves of English are tufts of Spanish, hardy and smelling of pupusas and ta- quitos and salsa verde he says he eats at least once a week at a restaurant in Spanish Harlem. No te preocupes, mamá, José Luis tells me, don't worry about me. I'm getting enough sleep, yes, I'm very careful when I walk across campus at night. . . . Of all my child's phases—jazz and photography, skiing competitions, and, last semester, Latin American novels—this is the one to fear and revere. A new language is a tincture, a drop of which forever changes the chemistry of the person who is learning it. He still talks about saving the planet—but now he seems to have found a point of departure—he tells me he will be volunteering next summer with a soil conser- vation project in El Salvador. It will be our first summer apart.

I remember the moment during our trip to El Salvador when he took his life in his hands and made something new out of it, although at the time I had no clue this was happening. After our day in the human rights office we were scheduled to visit Ciudad Grande, one of the settlements of repatriated refugees. I couldn't even think of it, I was so exhausted. I told José Luis I preferred to sit in the cathedral and pray and think and that he should do likewise, he should rest up before our trip home. Rest up. One of those lame, motherly admonitions that, more often than not, backfire. I could tell he was feeling guilty about not wanting to stay with me. And like a fool I let my need to control tick away a few seconds too long, and he saw through me and blew up. He said, I didn't come all this way to see my father's face—and not his world.

When he returned a day and a half later with Sister Margarita, he was in good spirits. Ma, hey, you'll never believe it. I met a family that's doing restoration work with traditional farming techniques. Can you believe they had their land seized by the army in the 1970s. . . . He spoke with the infinite passion of a young man who imagines he has discovered something new; of course, for him it was new, the story of El Salvador. Later, on the flight home, I noticed my son's face had changed, had traded in its hard edges for a more porous expression, something bordering on wonder. It was as if after having seen so many people who looked like him, he no longer had to bear the burden of his heritage by himself. He became free to explore new selves, new expressions. Now he tells me that he has been exchanging letters with the Salvadoran family's oldest daughter, Angela. She is his age. I don't know what this might mean, if anything. He is not one to admit, even to himself, that life has taken off in a new direction until long after the fact. And now all he can talk about is how much he enjoys writing Angela in Spanish and how much he looks forward to next summer. And I ache to think that we will be apart, I envy his ability to up and go at will, and I am bursting with pride at all he has become, strong and beautiful as a flowering cactus in the desert.

My baby, my son, beloved stranger, disappearing into a new language and landscape, leaving me to look inside myself for the magic I love in you. I am forty years old. I have melted down sadness and joy into a single blade with which to carve out a life. And I am just beginning to discern the shape that was there all along, just beginning to become me.

Epilogue

Ontario, Canada

Dear María,

I am sending this card to Soledad's
address with a prayer that it finds its way to
you. Yes, I went back. And then into hiding
for a very long time. Only recently has it been
safe enough for me to live in the light of day. I
heard through my contacts that you and a
young man came looking for me. If only I

could have known. Even though my reasons
for returning to my country were right, the act
of leaving you was never right. At the present
time I am visiting the Toronto Center for
War Survivors with the San Salvador
archbishop. We are talking with the directors
and looking for ways we can help refugees
return home when they are ready. Remember
that collection of poems I started? Well, I
finished them. And I hope you will approve of
my English translations. I have so many
stories to tell you, María. I pray you have not
forgotten me.

Your friend para siempre,
José Luis Alegría Cruz (y Romero)

Demetria Martínez lives in Tucson, Arizona, where she works as a columnist for the *National Catholic Reporter*. She was born and raised in Albuquerque, New Mexico, and received a B.A. from Princeton University.

In 1987 Martínez was indicted on charges related to smuggling Central American refugees into the United States. A jury later acquitted her on First Amendment grounds.

She is also the author of a collection of poetry, "Turning," included in the book *Three Times a Woman*.